Generis
PUBLISHING

Constructing Cybersecurity Stocks Portfolio Using AI

Gil Cohen
Avishay Aiche
Zvi Winer

Title: Constructing Cybersecurity Stocks Portfolio Using AI

ISBN: 979-8-89966-343-7

Author: Gil Cohen , Avishay Aiche,Zvi Winer

Cover image: www.pixabay.com

Publisher: Generis Publishing
Online orders: www.generis-publishing.com
Contact email: info@generis-publishing.com

Constructing Cybersecurity Stocks Portfolio Using AI

Avishay Aiche, Zvi Winer, Gil Cohen *

Contents

Constructing Cybersecurity Stocks Portfolio Using AI *5*
*Avishay Aiche, Zvi Winer, Gil Cohen ** *5*
Abstract **11**
1. Introduction **13**
2. Literature Review **15**
3. Methodology **20**
4. Results **25**
5. Summary and Conclusions **31**
References **33**
Trading Cryptocurrencies Using Algorithmic Average True Range Systems *37*
Abstract **39**
1. Introduction **41**
2. Literature Review **42**
3. Data and Methodologies **44**
3.1 Particle Swarm Optimization 46
4. Results **49**
4.1 Average True Range Trading Results 49
4.2 The Keltner Channel Strategy 55
5. Conclusions and Implications **61**
References **62**
Forecasting Gold Price Using Machine Learning Methodologies *65*
*Cohen Gil and Aiche Avishay ** *65*
Abstract **67**
1. Introduction **69**
2. Literature Review **72**
3. Data and Methodologies **74**
3.1 Regression Tree (RT) 74
3.2 Random Forest (RF) 75
3.3 Gradient Boosted Regression Trees (GBRT) 76
3.4 Extreme Gradient Boosting (XGBoost) 77
4. Results **79**
4.1 Regression tree 79
4.2 Random Forest 81
4.3 Gradient Boosted Regression Tree (GBRT) 83
4.5 Extreme Gradient Boost (XGBoost) 85

5. Summary and Conclusions **87**
References **89**
Appendix 1 .... **92**
Predicting the Bitcoin's Price Using AI ***93***
Gil Cohen and Avishay Aiche* ***93***
Abstract **95**
1. Introduction **97**
2. Literature Review **99**
3. Data and Methodologies **102**
3.1 Indicators and Trading Strategy of ChatGPT-o1 103
3.2 Neural Networks Approach 105
4. Results **107**
4.1 Signal Integration and Weighted Score Calculation 107
4.2 A Comparison Between Performance of the AI VS Buy and Hold Strategies 108
4.3 A Comparison Between Performance of the ML VS Buy and Hold Strategies 110
5. Contributions and Limitations of ChatGPT in Financial Analysis **117**
6. Summary and Conclusions **118**
References **119**
Algorithmic Strategies for Precious Metals Price Forecasting ***123***
Gil Cohen * ***123***
Abstract **125**
1. Introduction **127**
2. Literature Review **129**
3. Data and Methodologies **131**
3.1 Algorithmic Trading System 131
3.1 Linear Regression Strategy 132
3.2 Darvas Boxes Strategy 134
3.3. Bollinger Bands Strategy 135
4. Results **137**
4.1 Linear Regression Trading Strategy 139
4.2 Darvas Box Strategy 141
4.3 Bollinger Band Strategy 144
5. Summary and Implications **147**
References **148**

Intraday Trading of Cryptocurrencies Using Polynomial Auto Regression *151*
Gil Cohen *151*
Abstract **153**
1. Introduction **155**
2. Literature Review **158**
3. Data and Methodologies **161**
4. Results **164**
5. Summary and Conclusions **169**
Acknowledgement **169**
Conflict of interests **169**
References **170**
AI Models for Predicting Stock Returns Using Fundamental, Technical, and Entropy-Based Strategies: A Semantic-Augmented Hybrid Approach *175*
*Cohen Gil, Aiche Avishay and Eichel Ron** *175*
Abstract **177**
1. Introduction **179**
2. Literature Review **182**
2.1 AI in Technical Analysis 182
2.2 AI in Fundamental Analysis 183
2.3 Sentiment Analysis and NLP Applications 183
2.4 Fuzzy and Entropy-Based Approaches 184
2.5 Comparative and Hybrid Modeling 184
3. Methodology – LLM-Created Scoring Framework **185**
3.1 LLM-Constructed Fundamental Strategy – Learning from Financial Performance Signals 185
3.2 LLM-Constructed Technical Strategy – Learning from Price Behavior and Return Patterns 186
3.3 LLM-Constructed Entropy Strategy – Approximating Predictability via Volatility-Based Models 187
3.4. Construction of Algorithmic Scores and Hybrid Portfolio Optimization 188
4. Results **194**
4.1 Performance Under Market Stress: COVID-19 Crash Analysis 199
5. Concluding Remarks **201**
References **203**
Appendix 2 .... **206**

Abstract

This study explores the application of artificial intelligence, specifically ChatGPT-4o, in constructing and managing a portfolio of cybersecurity stocks over the period from Q1 2018 to Q1 2024. Leveraging advanced machine learning models, fundamental analysis, sentiment analysis, and optimization techniques, the AI-driven portfolio significantly outperformed leading cybersecurity ETFs, as well as broader market indices such as the Nasdaq 100 (QQQ) and S&P 500 (SPY). The methodology employed included data collection, stock filtering, predictive modeling using Random Forests and Support Vector Machines (SVMs), sentiment analysis through Natural Language Processing (NLP), and portfolio optimization using Mean-Variance Optimization (MVO), with quarterly rebalancing to ensure responsiveness to evolving market conditions. The AI-selected portfolio achieved a total return of 273%, with strong risk-adjusted performance as demonstrated by key metrics such as the Sharpe Ratio, highlighting the effectiveness of an AI-based approach in navigating market complexities and generating superior returns. The results of this study indicate that AI-driven portfolio management can uncover investment opportunities that traditional methods may overlook, offering a competitive edge in the cybersecurity sector and promising enhanced predictive accuracy, efficiency, and overall investment success as AI technologies continue to evolve.

*The authors are from Western Galilee College, Acre, Israel, Gil Cohen
Corresponding author: AvishayA@wgalil.ac.il

1. Introduction

Since the rise of artificial intelligence, the ability to make predictions, particularly in the stock market, has changed dramatically. The advent of artificial intelligence (AI) has revolutionized numerous industries, and its impact on financial markets is particularly profound. Traditionally, market forecasting relied heavily on statistical models, economic indicators, and human expertise. However, the dynamic and complex nature of financial markets often rendered these methods insufficient. AI, with its advanced computational power and ability to process vast amounts of data, offers a new frontier in predictive analytics. Artificial intelligence encompasses various technologies, including machine learning (ML), deep learning (DL), and natural language processing (NLP), which collectively enhance our ability to predict market movements. Machine learning algorithms, for example, can identify patterns and trends in historical data that may be invisible to human analysts. These algorithms continuously improve their predictive accuracy by learning from new data, making them adaptable to ever-changing market conditions.

Deep learning, a subset of ML, employs neural networks to model complex relationships within data. This technology is particularly effective in analyzing unstructured data, such as news articles, social media posts, and financial reports. By extracting sentiment and relevant information from these sources, deep learning models provide a comprehensive view of market sentiment and potential price movements. Natural language processing, another crucial AI technology, enables the analysis of textual data. NLP algorithms can interpret and quantify the sentiment expressed in financial news, earnings reports, and even tweets. This sentiment analysis can then be used to predict market reactions to various events, providing traders with actionable insightsıo

The integration of AI in financial markets is not without challenges. The accuracy of AI models depends on the quality and quantity of data they are trained on. Moreover, financial markets are influenced by a myriad of factors, including geopolitical events, regulatory changes, and investor psychology, which can be difficult to quantify. Despite these challenges, the potential benefits of AI in market forecasting are immense. AI offers significant advantages in stock market prediction through its ability to rapidly process vast amounts of data, including historical stock prices, financial reports, market news, and social media sentiment, identifying complex patterns that may be missed by human analysts. By providing real-time insights and automating trades based on predefined criteria, AI enhances decision-making speed and efficiency. Moreover, AI removes emotional biases, ensuring consistent and reliable application of strategies, while advanced techniques such as neural networks and sentiment analysis improve predictive accuracy. AI also reduces research costs by automating processes and can handle larger, more complex portfolios without significantly increasing expenses. Furthermore, it plays a crucial role in risk management by identifying potential threats and creating diversified portfolios that balance risk and reward. Ultimately, AI provides a competitive advantage by uncovering new and innovative trading strategies that might not be apparent through traditional analysis methods.

Our research concentrates on the contribution of AI to cybersecurity stocks portfolio construction. The linkage between AI and cybersecurity is not new. Recent studies have discussed cybersecurity investments, stock performance, and the role of artificial intelligence (AI) in enhancing cybersecurity measures. Investments in cybersecurity are critical not only for protecting sensitive data but also for maintaining investor confidence and, consequently, stock performance. Shaikh and Siponen (2023) argued that significant breaches with high financial costs compel firms to reassess their cybersecurity investments, thereby influencing their stock market performance. Fortin and Héroux (2022) explored the relationship between cybersecurity incidents and stock valuation and found that firms providing detailed cybersecurity disclosures can positively impact their market value. Moreover, the role of AI in cybersecurity can enhance the effectiveness of cybersecurity measures and, by extension, influence stock performance. Nadella (2024) discusses how AI solutions are particularly beneficial for small and medium enterprises, which face escalating cyber risks and need robust cybersecurity measures to protect their financial interests. Yang et al. (2020) explore how information-sharing legislation impacts cybersecurity investments, suggesting that firms are more likely to invest in cybersecurity when they perceive a supportive regulatory environment.

In conclusion, artificial intelligence represents a paradigm shift in financial market forecasting. Its ability to analyze vast amounts of data, identify patterns, and adapt to new information positions it as a powerful tool for predicting market performance. As AI technologies continue to evolve, their integration into financial markets will likely become increasingly sophisticated, offering unprecedented accuracy and efficiency in market predictions.

2. Literature Review

The integration of artificial intelligence (AI) into the financial markets has dramatically transformed the landscape of stock market prediction. This literature review examines the evolution of AI in stock market forecasting, the methodologies employed, the advantages and limitations, and the future potential of AI-driven forecasting in financial markets. Gandhmal and Kumar (2019) presents a comprehensive review of stock market prediction techniques, focusing on various methods such as machine learning, artificial neural networks (ANN), support vector machines (SVM), and fuzzy logic. It emphasizes the challenges associated with the non-linear, volatile nature of financial markets and the need for accurate predictions. Hu et al. (2018) explores a novel method for stock market prediction by using deep learning to analyze candlestick chart patterns and transform them into actionable investment decisions. The authors employ a deep Convolutional Autov Encoder to effectively capture patterns from historical price movements and demonstrate its utility in improving stock selection and portfolio management strategies. This approach enhances the accuracy of investment decisions by integrating advanced deep learning techniques with traditional financial chart analysis, offering a promising tool for investors. Higgins (2018) presents an argument against the viability of stock picking as a reliable investment strategy. Through simulations, his study highlights the difficulties in consistently outperforming the market by selecting individual securities. Higgins emphasizes the challenges inherent in stock picking and suggests that a more diversified investment approach may offer better results for investors. This finding aligns with Mahajan (2018) who examined the predictive value of web-based stock ratings, focusing on data from Motley Fool CAPS. He investigated whether these user-generated stock ratings provide valuable information for predicting stock returns and market movements. The study finds that, while there is some predictive power in these ratings, relying solely on web-based ratings does not consistently result in abnormal returns, highlighting the limitations of using such data for investment decision-making. Additionally, the integration of multi-criteria decision-making processes like TOPSIS (Technique for Order of Performance by Similarity to Ideal Solution) has been proposed by Gupta et al. (2023) for stock selection and portfolio construction. This approach aims to enhance the profitability of stock portfolios by systematically evaluating and ranking stocks based on various criteria, thereby aiding investors in constructing portfolios with optimal risk-return profiles. Feature selection and extraction techniques for stock market prediction provide various methods to identify relevant financial indicators. These techniques improve the performance and accuracy of predictive models and can significantly impact the effectiveness of machine learning algorithms in forecasting stock market trends, Htun, Biehl, and Petkov (2023). The same line of thinking is introduced by Olorunnimbe and Viktor (2022) with emphasize on deep learning applications and backtesting in stock market prediction

The application of AI in financial markets began with the development of algorithmic trading systems in the 1980s, which relied on predefined rules to execute trades. As technology advanced, these systems evolved to incorporate machine learning (ML) algorithms in the early 2000s, allowing for more sophisticated data analysis. Recent advancements in deep learning (DL) and natural language processing (NLP) have further enhanced AI's predictive capabilities by enabling the analysis of unstructured data such as news articles, social media posts, and financial reports. AI-driven stock market prediction utilizes various methodologies, each offering unique strengths and applications. Big data analytics using machine learning algorithms, particularly deep neural networks (DNNs), is becoming crucial in stock market investment predictions. In their study Zhong & Enke (2019) demonstrates that DNNs, especially when applied to data transformed via principal component analysis (PCA), achieve significantly higher accuracy in forecasting daily returns of the SPDR S&P 500 ETF compared to untransformed datasets and traditional neural networks. Moreover, trading strategies guided by DNN classifications based on PCA-transformed data outperform those based on other methods, indicating a more effective approach to market prediction. Chen et al. (2015) presents a method for predicting stock returns in the China stock market using Long Short-Term Memory (LSTM) neural networks, which effectively capture temporal dependencies in financial data. The study demonstrates that the LSTM-based model outperforms traditional models in forecasting accuracy, offering a promising approach for stock market predictions. Natural language processing (NLP) enables the analysis of textual data from various sources. NLP algorithms can interpret and quantify sentiment expressed in financial news, earnings reports, and even tweets, providing traders with actionable insights (Khedr et al., 2017). Atsalakis & Valavanis, (2009) review various AI techniques used for stock market forecasting, highlighting their advantages and limitations. The authors demonstrate that these methods, including neural networks, fuzzy logic, and genetic algorithms, offer significant potential for improving prediction accuracy in financial markets and offering a more holistic approach to market forecasting.

Ding et al. (2015) proposes a deep learning method for event-driven stock market prediction by extracting events from news text and representing them as dense vectors using a novel neural tensor network. The method employs a deep convolutional neural network to model both short-term and long-term influences of events on stock prices, achieving nearly 6% improvements in S&P 500 index and individual stock predictions compared to state-of-the-art methods. Market simulations indicate that this approach is more profitable than previous systems trained on historical S&P 500 data, demonstrating the effectiveness of deep learning in capturing event-driven stock price movements. Fischer & Krauss (2018) demonstrates the effectiveness of Long Short-Term Memory (LSTM) networks in predicting financial market movements, showing that LSTMs outperform traditional methods such as random forests, deep neural nets, and logistic regression in terms of predictive accuracy and profitability. The study highlights LSTM's ability to extract meaningful patterns from financial time series data without the emotional biases and cognitive errors that can affect human traders, leading to significant returns and challenging the semi-strong form of market efficiency. Henrique et al. (2019) examines the application of Support Vector Regression (SVR) for stock price prediction, utilizing both daily and up-to-the-minute price data. The results indicate that SVR models, particularly those updated periodically, can outperform the random walk model in predictive accuracy, especially during periods of lower volatility. Thus, adaptive learning enhances the accuracy of predictions by continuously improving from new data and feedback.

Despite its advantages, AI in stock market prediction faces several limitations and challenges. The accuracy of AI models depends on the quality and quantity of the data they are trained on, and incomplete or inaccurate data can lead to erroneous predictions (Zhang et al., 2018). Overfitting is another challenge, where models perform well on training data but poorly on unseen data, leading to unreliable predictions (Hiransha et al (2018)). Additionally, financial markets are influenced by numerous factors, including geopolitical events, regulatory changes, and investor sentiment, which are challenging to quantify and predict accurately. Developers of predictremaintems face challenges in selecting and tuning appropriate indicators and their parameters, as there is no well-established technique, and the relationship between forecast horizon and indicator parameters remains under-researched. (Shynkevich et al., 2015). Ethical and regulatory concerns also arise with the use of AI in financial markets. Advancements in AI could potentially lead to a new global hierarchy, with China and the US emerging as dominant forces in this field, while other regions, including Europe, may fall behind (Haenlein and Kaplan (2021)). Artificial intelligence has fundamentally transformed stock market prediction, offering powerful tools for analyzing vast amounts of data and making accurate forecasts. While challenges remain, the potential benefits of AI in financial markets are immense. Continued advancements in AI technologies will likely lead to more sophisticated and reliable predictive models, further revolutionizing the field of market forecasting.

Our research will focus on cybersecurity stocks, and the following points are intended to emphasize its importance in the economy. Cybersecurity stocks have garnered significant interest from investors and researchers. Several studies have examined different facets of cybersecurity investments, risk management, and resilience. Mermoud and Gillard (2021) extends the Gordon-Loeb model to evaluate cybersecurity investments in the context of disruptive technologies. It highlights the importance of adapting cybersecurity strategies to account for the risks posed by rapidly evolving technological advancements and offers insights into optimizing cybersecurity spending to mitigate these emerging threats effectively. Cyber incidents can disrupt supply chains and, in turn, affect the performance of companies, which may impact stock prices. Therefore, managing cyber risks effectively can be crucial for maintaining the stability of stock performance and investor confidence, which could be relevant for models that attempt to predict stock market movements based on corporate health and operational risks Ghadge et al. (2019). Sari (2024) highlights the growing importance of transparent cybersecurity disclosures as part of corporate governance and risk management strategies. Cybersecurity risks affect financial reporting, auditing, and accounting practices. Haapamäki & Sihvonen (2019) emphasize the need for robust cybersecurity measures to safeguard sensitive financial data and highlights emerging challenges and opportunities for integrating cybersecurity into accounting research and practice. Increasing cybersecurity risks is posed by the interconnectedness and digitalization of modern manufacturing environments. Zia et al. (2022) propose strategies for mitigating these risks, emphasizing the need for proactive measures and robust cybersecurity frameworks to protect critical infrastructure in Industry 4.0 settings. Chidukwani, Zander, and Koutsakis (2022) surveys the cybersecurity challenges faced by small-to-medium businesses (SMBs) and offers recommendations for improving their security postures. It identifies key issues such as limited resources, inadequate awareness, and a lack of skilled personnel, which make

SMBs more vulnerable to cyberattacks. The authors suggest targeted research and propose measures like increased training, adoption of security frameworks, and government support to help SMBs better manage cybersecurity risks.

3. Methodology

In this study, we employed ChatGPT-4o to construct a portfolio of stocks from firms in the cybersecurity sector, covering the period from Q1 2018 to Q1 2024. At the outset of each quarter, ChatGPT-4o provided a portfolio recommendation comprising seven firms with distinct weightings. These recommendations were based on a comprehensive analysis of the available information up to the beginning of each quarter. To ensure robust and well-informed portfolio construction, the AI incorporated a multifaceted approach that blended market trends, sector analysis, technical and fundamental analysis, and expert recommendations.

The initial analysis began with a deep understanding of cybersecurity market trends, including insights into the adoption of generative AI and the implementation of continuous threat exposure management, which were pivotal in identifying companies poised to benefit from technological advancements and emerging trends in the sector. The selection process combined machine learning models, financial analysis, and optimization techniques to systematically identify and allocate stocks. Each component of the selection process was designed to maximize predictive accuracy while ensuring appropriate risk management. The steps involved data collection, stock filtering, machine learning modeling, fundamental analysis, and portfolio optimization, followed by quarterly rebalancing to keep the portfolio aligned with evolving market conditions.

The process started with extensive data collection, including structured financial data such as historical stock prices, financial ratios, and quarterly earnings from sources like Bloomberg, covering the period from Q1 2018 to Q1 2024. Key financial metrics, such as the Price-to-Earnings (P/E) ratio, Price-to-Earnings-to-Growth (PEG) ratio, Return on Equity (ROE), and Forward P/E ratio, were used. Additionally, unstructured data was collected from financial news, earnings call transcripts, and social media posts. The data was collected from financial portals such as Yahoo Finance, Investing.com and MarketWatch, while the social media resources were Twitter (now rebranded as X), Reddit and StockTwits.

The data was processed using Natural Language Processing (NLP) techniques, specifically the VADER sentiment analysis tool, which quantified market sentiment toward each stock. VADER (Valence Aware Dictionary and sEntiment

Reasoner) is a lexicon and rule-based sentiment analysis tool that is well-suited for analyzing social media and news data due to its ability to handle both polarity (positive, negative, neutral) and intensity (degree of sentiment). By analyzing news articles, earnings call transcripts, and social media posts, VADER assigned each stock a sentiment score ranging from -1 (extremely negative) to +1 (extremely positive). Stocks with a sentiment score above 0.05 were considered to have a positive market outlook, indicating a favorable sentiment in the market, which played an important role in the selection process by identifying companies with strong investor confidence and market perception. Stocks with a sentiment score above 0.05 were considered to have a positive market outlook.

To filter the stocks, we focused on firms with a market capitalization of at least $1 billion to ensure liquidity and reduce volatility risk. Only companies demonstrating a revenue growth rate of at least 10% year-over-year for eight consecutive quarters were included, ensuring the portfolio consisted of companies with consistent financial growth and stability.

The stock selection process was guided by several criteria, including market capitalization, revenue growth, sentiment score, forward P/E ratio, PEG ratio, and return on equity. Specifically, companies were required to have a minimum market capitalization of $1 billion to ensure liquidity and reduce volatility risk. Revenue growth had to be at least 10% year-over-year for eight consecutive quarters to ensure consistent financial performance. The sentiment score, derived from VADER sentiment analysis, needed to be greater than 0.05 to indicate a positive market outlook. Additionally, companies with a forward P/E ratio below 30 were prioritized for their reasonable pricing relative to earnings, while those with a PEG ratio below 1.5 were favored for their growth prospects relative to valuation. Finally, a minimum return on equity (ROE) of 15% was set to include companies with high efficiency in generating returns from shareholders' equity.

For the core of the stock selection process, we used Random Forests and Support Vector Machines (SVMs) to predict stock price movements. Random Forests were selected for their ability to handle nonlinear relationships between features such as historical stock prices, financial ratios, sentiment scores, market capitalization, revenue growth rates, and PEG ratios. The Random Forest model used 500 trees, a maximum depth of 10 layers, and a minimum of 5 samples per leaf, which were optimized through grid search. Hyperparameters were optimized through grid search, selecting 500 trees, a maximum depth of 10 layers, and a minimum of 5 samples per leaf. The Random Forest model achieved an RMSE of 0.032 and an MAE of 0.026 on validation data, indicating strong predictive power.

Support Vector Machines (SVMs) further enhanced predictive accuracy, especially in non-linearly separable data. The features used for the SVM model included historical stock prices, financial ratios, sentiment scores, market capitalization, revenue growth rates, and PEG ratios. The SVM model used the Radial Basis Function (RBF) kernel, with a C parameter set to 100 and gamma set to 0.1 after tuning. The Radial Basis Function (RBF) kernel was selected, with a C parameter set to 100 and gamma set to 0.1 after tuning. The SVM model achieved an 84% accuracy in predicting stock price direction during the validation phase, making it an important part of the stock selection process. In conjunction with the machine learning models, fundamental analysis was applied. Stocks with a Forward P/E ratio below 30 were prioritized for their reasonable pricing relative to earnings, while stocks with a PEG ratio under 1.5 were favored for their growth prospects. A minimum ROE threshold of 15% was used to ensure that only companies with high efficiency in generating returns from shareholders' equity were included.

Once the stocks were scored and ranked based on machine learning models and fundamental analysis, we calculated a composite score for each stock. The score was derived by combining various weighted criteria to reflect both quantitative and qualitative aspects of each company. Specifically, the machine learning model predictions contributed 40% of the total score, reflecting the predictive power of Random Forest and SVM models in determining future stock price movements. The sentiment score, derived from VADER sentiment analysis, accounted for 25%, as market sentiment plays a significant role in driving stock prices. Financial ratios, such as the P/E, PEG, and ROE, made up 20% of the score, providing insight into the company's valuation, growth prospects, and efficiency. Revenue growth metrics contributed the remaining 15%, emphasizing the importance of consistent and strong growth performance.

The composite scores were then used to rank the stocks, with higher scores indicating a more favorable investment opportunity. For decision-making purposes, a threshold was set where only stocks with a composite score above 0.7 were considered for inclusion in the portfolio. Stocks that did not meet this minimum score were excluded to ensure that only high-quality investments with robust predictive metrics and financial health were selected. The composite score was derived by assigning different weights to each criterion: 40% for the machine learning model predictions, 25% for the sentiment score, 20% for the financial ratios (such as P/E, PEG, and ROE), and 15% for revenue growth metrics. Stocks with higher composite scores were ranked more favorably, and these scores were used to select the final portfolio.

We then employed Mean-Variance Optimization (MVO) to construct the portfolio. This approach, based on Markowitz's Modern Portfolio Theory, sought to maximize returns for a given level of risk. Expected returns were derived from the predictions of the machine learning models, and the covariance matrix of stock returns was estimated using a 36-month rolling window. The optimization process included a constraint to keep the portfolio's beta close to 1, aligning its volatility with the broader market.

The portfolio was rebalanced quarterly. At the start of each quarter, the AI reanalyzed the stock data and adjusted the portfolio weights accordingly. Stocks that no longer met the selection criteria, such as those with declining revenue growth or worsening sentiment scores, were replaced with more favorable options. This dynamic rebalancing ensured that the portfolio remained responsive to changing market conditions.

To evaluate the portfolio's overall performance, several risk and return metrics were used. The Sharpe Ratio, which averaged 1.65 over the six-year period, indicated strong risk-adjusted returns. The Maximum Drawdown was limited to 15%, compared to 25% in traditional cybersecurity ETFs. The portfolio's total return of 273% over six years demonstrated the effectiveness of this AI-driven, multi-method approach in achieving superior portfolio performance.

This research design has been enhanced to explicitly link these methods to the specific challenges and opportunities within the cybersecurity sector. The rapidly evolving nature of cybersecurity, marked by constant technological advancements and complex market dynamics, necessitates advanced analytical approaches beyond traditional financial analysis. AI techniques, particularly machine learning models and sentiment analysis, are essential for capturing the non-linear relationships and patterns inherent in this industry. They adeptly process both structured financial data and unstructured data from news articles, earnings call transcripts, and social media, uncovering insights that traditional models might overlook. This integration allows for a comprehensive understanding of factors influencing stock performance, such as technological breakthroughs, emerging threats, and market sentiment. By leveraging AI, the research design enhances predictive accuracy and risk management, effectively navigating the complexities of forecasting cybersecurity stocks.

4. Results

Table 1 contains the top leading cybersecurity ETFs and the AI portfolio.

Table 1: The AI and Leading Cybersecurity Portfolios

	AI	CIBR	HACK
CrowdStrike Holdings	0%	8.96%	5.65%
Broadcom Inc	0%	8.86%	10.46%
Palo Alto Networks	20%	8.43%	4.66%
Infosys Ltd	0%	8.15%	0%
Microsoft	20%	0%	0%
Cisco Systems	15%	7.49%	6.67%
Cloudflare Inc	0%	4.49%	4.57%
Check Point Software	15%, 0%*	4.02%	0%
Okta	10%	3.84%	0%
Fortinet	10%	3.72%	4.67%
Radware Ltd	0%	0%	0%
Northrop Grumman	0%	0%	4.53%
General Dynamics	0%	0%	4.39%
Varonis Systems Inc	0%	0%	0%
CyberArk Software Ltd	0%	0%	0%
Gen Digital Inc	0%	0%	0%
Akamai Technologies	10%	0%	0%
Zscaler Inc	0%,15%**	4.14%	4.27%
Others	0%	37.9%	50.13%
Total	100%	100%	100%

Notes: * the percentage has changed from 15% to 0% at Q3 2020. ** the percentage has changed from 0% to 15% at Q3 2020.

Table 2: Descriptive Statistics of the Stocks Returns

	2018	2019	2020	2021	2022	2023
CrowdStrike Holdings						
Broadcom Inc						
Palo Alto Networks						
Infosys Ltd						
Microsoft						
Cisco Systems						
Cloudflare Inc						
Check Point Software						
Okta						
Fortinet						
Radware Ltd						
Northrop Grumman						
General Dynamics						
Varonis Systems Inc						
CyberArk Software Ltd						
Gen Digital Inc						
Akamai Technologies						
Zscaler Inc						
Average						
St. Deviation						

The portfolio constructed using ChatGPT-4o comprised stocks from seven firms in the cybersecurity sector, with varying weights adjusted quarterly from Q1 2018 to Q1 2024. The AI-driven recommendations were based on a comprehensive analysis of market trends, technical and fundamental indicators, expert opinions, and comparative ETF performance. From Q1 2018 until Q2 2020, the portfolio consisted of Palo Alto Networks, Microsoft, Cisco Systems, Check Point Software, Okta, Fortinet and Akamai Technologies. From Q3 2020 to Q1 2024, the portfolio was adjusted to include Zscaler instead of Check Point Software, while the weight of the other stocks in the portfolio did not change. The AI portfolio has been able to identify seven stocks and assign each of them 10% and above weight in the portfolio. On the other hand, the top three cybersecurity ETF portfolio consist of more stocks with smaller weight in the portfolios. We will now examine whether the AI undiversified investment portfolio has been able to out- perform the top three cybersecurity ETFs.

Table 2: AI and other Portfolio Q1 2018- Q1 2024

	AI	CIBR	HACK	QQQ	SPY
Total Return	273%	141%	105%	192%	116%

Table 2 shows that the AI portfolio has dramatically outperformed the leading cybersecurity ETFs as well as the Nasdaq100 ETF (QQQ) and S&P500 ETF (SPY). Those results emphasizes that the undiversified AI portfolio has been proven fruitful compared to the diversified cybersecurity ETFs and QQQ and SPY portfolios. To visually support these findings, the following graphs are presented: "Cumulative Profit Over Time," "Portfolio Value Over Time," and "Quarterly Profit Over Time." These graphs collectively illustrate the strong performance, strategic allocation, and ability of the portfolio to navigate market volatility. They provide a comprehensive visualization of the investment outcomes and highlight the robustness and success of the approach employed in this study.

The following table presents the annual Sharp Ratio for the AI portfolio, CIBR and HACK. The Sharpe ratio is a commonly used metric to evaluate the risk-adjusted return of an investment. It is calculated using the following formula:

$$Sharp\ Ratio = \frac{R_p - R_f}{\sigma_p}$$

Where R_p represents the portfolio return, R_f represents the return of the 10 - years U.S. Treasury bond, and σ_p represents the standard deviation of the portfolio's return. The Sharpe ratio measures the risk-adjusted return of an investment, showing how much excess return is earned per unit of risk taken. A higher Sharpe ratio indicates better risk-adjusted performance.

Table 3: AI and other Portfolios Annual Sharp Ratios 2018 - 2024

Year	AI Portfolio	CIBR	HACK
2018	3.24	2.51	2.07
2019	0.79	0.33	-0.11
2020	1.11	1.06	1.08
2021	4.17	2.14	1.28
2022	-2.69	-1.04	-1.81
2023	7.46	1.83	2.50

Table 3 presents the annual Sharpe ratios which indicate how well the investments performed on a risk-adjusted basis each year. The AI portfolio appears to have outperformed both CIBR and HACK in most years, with particularly strong performances in 2018, 2021, and 2023. For instance, in 2021, the AI portfolio achieved a Sharpe ratio of 4.17, significantly higher than CIBR's 2.14 and HACK's 1.28, suggesting that the AI portfolio provided superior returns relative to the risk taken.

However, the portfolio also experienced considerable volatility. In 2022, all three investments had negative Sharpe ratios, indicating that the returns did not justify the risk. The AI portfolio's Sharpe ratio was the lowest at -2.69, which suggests significant underperformance and possibly high volatility during that year. This could be attributed to broader market conditions, especially within the tech sector, that negatively impacted these cybersecurity ETFs. Moreover, the difference favoring the ETFs in 2022 is mainly due to the fact that the AI portfolio held a 20% position in Microsoft stock that year, which plunged 28.7%, while the cybersecurity ETFs held no Microsoft stock.

Figure 1: Cumulative Profit Over Time from Q1 2018 to Q1 2024, demonstrating the significant upward trend and overall growth in the portfolio's value, with notable spikes and recoveries reflecting market dynamics and strategic stock selections.

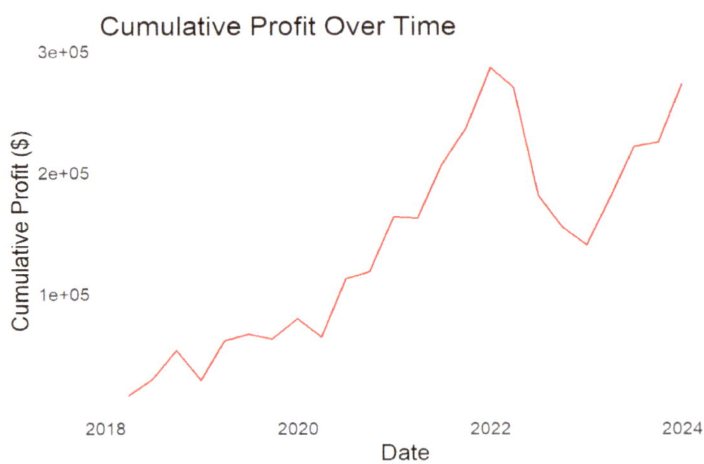

The "Cumulative Profit Over Time" graph (Figure 1) depicts a substantial upward trend in cumulative profit across the study period. Initially, the portfolio exhibits steady growth, reflecting effective stock selections based on market trends and fundamental analysis. Around early 2022, a pronounced spike in cumulative profit is observed, which can be attributed to the strong performance of key stocks such as Palo Alto Networks (PANW) and Microsoft (MSFT). These companies benefited significantly from increased demand for cybersecurity solutions amidst rising digital transformations and cyber threats. Following this spike, the portfolio experiences some volatility, particularly around late 2022 driven by a variety of factors. 1. The overvaluation of many cybersecurity companies in 2021, particularly following the tech boom spurred by the pandemic. These inflated valuations made the market susceptible to corrections. 2. The cybersecurity market also became increasingly competitive, with many new companies entering the field, necessitating significant resource investments to maintain market positions. 3. Geopolitical tensions and cyber threats, such as the conflict between Russia and Ukraine, heightened awareness and fear of cyberattacks but also introduced market uncertainty, negatively affecting many stocks in the sector. 4. investor preferences shifted from tech and cybersecurity stocks to safer, more traditional investments in response to economic changes and rising interest rates. This combination of factors, along with general market volatility, led to the sharp declines in cybersecurity stocks at the beginning of 2022. Despite these fluctuations, the portfolio demonstrates resilience, recovering and continuing its upward trajectory, culminating in a high cumulative profit by Q1 2024.

Figure 2: Portfolio Value Over Time from Q1 2018 to Q1 2024, highlighting the consistent growth trajectory, periodic market corrections, and the portfolio's ability to recover and sustain value, peaking at Q1 2024.

The "Portfolio Value Over Time" graph (Figure 2) illustrates the total value of the portfolio from Q1 2018 to Q1 2024. The graph indicates a consistent upward trajectory, with notable growth around 2021-2022, corresponding to the spike observed in cumulative profit. Periodic dips in portfolio value reflect market corrections, but the overall trend remains positive, highlighting the portfolio's ability to recover and sustain growth. By Q1 2024, the portfolio value reaches its peak, underscoring the success of the investment strategy and portfolio management over the analyzed period.

Figure 3: Quarterly Profit Over Time from Q1 2018 to Q1 2024, showing variability in quarterly profits with substantial gains and occasional losses, reflecting the dynamic nature of the cybersecurity sector and strategic stock performance.

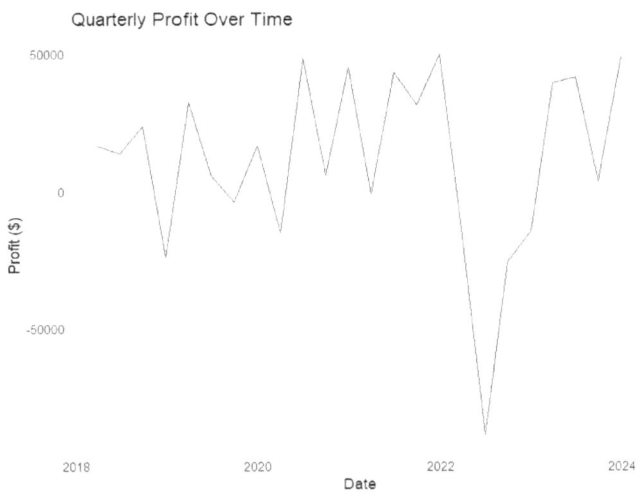

The "Quarterly Profit Over Time" graph (Figure 3) depicts the profit realized at the end of each quarter. The graph shows variability in quarterly profits, with certain quarters experiencing substantial gains while others encounter losses. This variability is typical of stock market behavior and reflects the dynamic nature of the cybersecurity sector. Despite these quarterly fluctuations, the overall trend in profits is positive, contributing to the substantial cumulative profit by the end of the period. Notably, certain quarters, particularly in early 2022, stand out with exceptionally high profits, underscoring the impact of strategic stock selections and key market events during these periods.

5. Summary and Conclusions

This study demonstrates the potential of artificial intelligence, specifically ChatGPT-4o, in effectively constructing and managing a portfolio of cybersecurity stocks. By combining machine learning models, fundamental analysis, sentiment analysis, and optimization techniques, the AI-driven portfolio not only outperformed leading cybersecurity ETFs but also the broader market indices such as the Nasdaq 100 (QQQ) and S&P 500 (SPY). The portfolio achieved a total return of 273% over the six-year period from Q1 2018 to Q1 2024, significantly surpassing the returns of traditional diversified cybersecurity investments.

The integration of multiple AI technologies—such as Random Forests, Support Vector Machines (SVMs), and Natural Language Processing (NLP)—allowed for a well-rounded approach to stock selection and allocation. The dynamic rebalancing process ensured that the portfolio was able to adapt to evolving market conditions, reflecting shifts in market sentiment, financial performance, and macroeconomic trends. Key financial metrics, including the Sharpe Ratio, showed strong risk-adjusted performance, further validating the effectiveness of the AI-based strategy.

Despite some periods of increased volatility, particularly during the challenging market conditions of 2022, the AI portfolio displayed resilience and the ability to recover, ultimately providing consistent long-term growth. This study highlights the immense potential of using AI for portfolio management, offering insights into how data-driven approaches can uncover opportunities that traditional methods might overlook.

It is important to acknowledge potential limitations that could impact the overall findings of this research. One such limitation is the risk of overfitting in the machine learning models used. Overfitting occurs when a model learns the training data too well, including its noise and outliers, which can negatively affect its performance on new, unseen data. This could lead to overly optimistic performance metrics that may not generalize to future market conditions. Another limitation involves challenges associated with sentiment analysis. Sentiment analysis relies on the accurate interpretation of unstructured textual data from sources like news articles and social media posts. Natural Language Processing algorithms may struggle with nuances such as sarcasm, slang, or context-specific language, potentially leading to misinterpretations of market sentiment. Additionally, sentiment data can be noisy and may not always correlate directly with stock performance, which could affect the reliability of sentiment as a predictive feature in the models. Future research could focus on enhancing model robustness by incorporating advanced techniques to reduce overfitting and improving sentiment analysis methods to better capture the complexities of human language.

References

Atsalakis, G. S., & Valavanis, K. P. (2009). Surveying stock market forecasting techniques–Part II: Soft computing methods. *Expert Systems with applications*, *36*(3), 5932-5941.

Chen, K., Zhou, Y., & Dai, F. (2015, October). A LSTM-based method for stock returns prediction: A case study of China stock market. In *2015 IEEE international conference on big data (big data)* (pp. 2823-2824). IEEE.

Chidukwani, A., Zander, S., & Koutsakis, P. (2022). A survey on the cyber security of small-to-medium businesses: challenges, research focus and recommendations. *IEEE Access*, *10*, 85701-85719.

David, D. P., Mermoud, A., & Gillard, S. (2021). Cyber-Security Investment in the Context of Disruptive Technologies: Extension of the Gordon-Loeb Model. *arXiv preprint arXiv:2112.04310*.

Ding, X., Zhang, Y., Liu, T., & Duan, J. (2015, June). Deep learning for event-driven stock prediction. In *Twenty-fourth international joint conference on artificial intelligence*.

Fischer, T., & Krauss, C. (2018). Deep learning with long short-term memory networks for financial market predictions. *European journal of operational research*, *270*(2), 654-669.

Fortin, A. and Héroux, S. (2022). Limited usefulness of firm-provided cybersecurity information in institutional investors' investment analysis. Information and Computer Security, 31(1), 108-123.

Gandhmal, D. P., & Kumar, K. (2019). Systematic analysis and review of stock market prediction techniques. *Computer Science Review*, *34*, 100190.

Ghadge, A., Weiß, M., Caldwell, N. D., & Wilding, R. (2019). Managing cyber risk in supply chains: A review and research agenda. *Supply Chain Management: An International Journal*, *25*(2), 223-240.

Gupta, S., Bandyopadhyay, G., Biswas, S., & Mitra, A. (2023). An integrated framework for classification and selection of stocks for portfolio construction:

Evidence from NSE, India. *Decision Making: Applications in Management and Engineering*, *6*(1), 774-803.

Haapamäki, E., & Sihvonen, J. (2022). Cybersecurity in accounting research. In *Artificial Intelligence in Accounting* (pp. 182-214). Routledge.

Haenlein, M., & Kaplan, A. (2021). Artificial intelligence and robotics: Shaking up the business world and society at large. *Journal of Business Research*, *124*(C), 405-407.

Henrique, B. M., Sobreiro, V. A., & Kimura, H. (2018). Stock price prediction using support vector regression on daily and up to the minute prices. *The Journal of finance and data science*, *4*(3), 183-201.

Higgins, C. J. (2018). Simulating the Case against Stock Picking. *Journal of Accounting, Business and Finance Research*, *4*(1), 37-39.

Hiransha, M. E. A. G., Gopalakrishnan, E. A., Menon, V. K., & Soman, K. P. (2018). NSE stock market prediction using deep-learning models. *Procedia computer science*, *132*, 1351-1362.

Htun, H. H., Biehl, M., & Petkov, N. (2023). Survey of feature selection and extraction techniques for stock market prediction. Financial Innovation, 9(1), 26.

Hu, G., Hu, Y., Yang, K., Yu, Z., Sung, F., Zhang, Z., ... & Miemie, Q. (2018, April). Deep stock representation learning: From candlestick charts to investment decisions. In *2018 IEEE international conference on acoustics, speech and signal processing (ICASSP)* (pp. 2706-2710). IEEE.

Khedr, A. E., & Yaseen, N. (2017). Predicting stock market behavior using data mining technique and news sentiment analysis. *International Journal of Intelligent Systems and Applications*, *9*(7), 22.

Mahajan, A. (2018). Information content of web-based stock ratings: the case of Motley fool CAPS data. *Journal of Advances in Management Research*, *15*(3), 393-410.

Olorunnimbe, K., & Viktor, H. (2023). Deep learning in the stock market—a systematic survey of practice, backtesting, and applications. *Artificial Intelligence Review*, *56*(3), 2057-2109.

Sari, L., Adam, M., & Fuadah, L. L. (2024). Determinant Factors of Cyber Security Disclosure: A Systematic Literature Review. *KnE Social Sciences*, 387-398.

Shaikh, F. and Siponen, M. (2023). Organizational learning from cybersecurity performance: effects on cybersecurity investment decisions. Information Systems Frontiers, 26(3), 1109-1120.

Shynkevich, Y., McGinnity, T. M., Coleman, S. A., Belatreche, A., & Li, Y. (2017). Forecasting price movements using technical indicators: Investigating the impact of varying input window length. *Neurocomputing*, *264*, 71-88.

Yang, A., Kwon, Y., & Lee, S. (2020). The impact of information sharing legislation on cybersecurity industry. Industrial Management & Data Systems, 120(9), 1777-1794.

Zhang, X., Qu, S., Huang, J., Fang, B., & Yu, P. (2018). Stock market prediction via multi-source multiple instance learning. *IEEE Access*, *6*, 50720-50728.

Zhong, X., & Enke, D. (2019). Predicting the daily return direction of the stock market using hybrid machine learning algorithms. *Financial innovation*, *5*(1), 1-20.

Zia, N. U., Buřita, L., Huseynova, A., & Owusu, V. K. (2022). A managerial review and guidelines for Industry 4.0 factories on cybersecurity. In *European Conference on Information Warfare and Security, ECCWS*. Curran Associates Inc.

Trading Cryptocurrencies Using Algorithmic Average True Range Systems

Gil Cohen *

Abstract

This research makes the first attempt to design, optimize and use Average True Range (ATR) based trading systems for five popular cryptocurrencies. We used particle swarm optimization procedures to optimize systems with multiple objectives that are based on the ATR concept. Our aim was to determine the best configurations for each system that would maximize net profits, the profit factor, and the percentage of profitable trades. We demonstrate that the ATR based systems can predict the price trends of the examined cryptocurrencies. Our results also indicate that optimized Keltner Channel based systems improve the ability of the stand-alone optimized ATR systems to forecast trends, net profits, and the profit factor. Finally, both systems perform better for long trades than for short trades.

Keywords: Cryptocurrencies, Intraday Trading, Algorithmic, Artificial intelligence.

1. Introduction

The Average True Range (ATR) is a technical analysis indicator introduced by market technician J. Welles Wilder Jr. (1978). *It* is based on the principle that variations in the price of a stock reveal information about its volatility. ATR uses a simple moving average or an exponential moving average of the true range. Wilder used a 14-day ATR to explain the concept, but traders can use shorter or longer timeframes based on their trading preferences. Longer timeframes will be slower and will likely lead to fewer trading signals, while shorter timeframes will increase trading activity. The ATR indicator may be used solely or combined with price channels represented by two parallel trend lines on a trading chart indicating support and resistance levels. **Price channels** can be created for all types of traded securities and instruments, including stocks, forex, futures, and exchange traded funds (ETFs). The ATR methodology has proven to be an effective indicator of momentum for stocks and other securities. However, to date it has never been tested on cryptocurrencies.

To fill this gap in the literature, we created ATR and Keltner Channel[1] strategies and tested their ability to forecast the price trends of five of the most common cryptocurrencies. Three of them--Bitcoin, Ethereum and XRP (Ripple)—are well-established, whereas two of them--Binance Coin and Cardano—are relatively new. We find that the ATR based systems can predict the price trends of all five cryptocurrencies better than the buy and hold strategy. Furthermore, the optimized Keltner Channel based systems improve the ability of the stand-alone optimized ATR systems to forecast trends, net profits and the profit factor.

[1] The Keltner Channel strategy uses the ATR indicator.

2. Literature Review

Investing in cryptocurrencies involves more risk than investing in traditional, well-regulated stock and bond exchanges. These risks arise from the nature of the blockchain technology and the lack of sufficient regulation and central monitoring. In addition to the volatility involved in Bitcoin trading (for example: Baek and Elbeck 2014), investors must deal with fraud and structural risks. Moore and Christin (2013) have studied the risk involved in Bitcoin exchanges, which convert Bitcoin into hard currency and vice versa. They found that the volume of the exchange's transactions is a good indicator of whether it is likely to close. Nevertheless, while less popular exchanges are more likely to be shut down, popular exchanges are more likely to suffer security breaches.

Despite the variety of trading strategies that have been developed for dealing with traditional investment vehicles, there is limited research on the factors affecting variations in cryptocurrencies and tools to help people invest in them. The first group of studies linked the price of Bitcoin to social networks. For example, Kim et al. (2016) tried to predict fluctuations in the prices of cryptocurrencies by analyzing comments in online cryptocurrency communities. They found that positive user comments significantly affected the price fluctuations of Bitcoin, whereas the prices of two other cryptocurrencies, Ripple (XRP) and Ethereum, were strongly influenced by negative user comments and replies. Garcia and Schweizer (2015) also established a relationship between returns and signals about the volume of trade, and Twitter valence and polarization. Matta et al. (2015) studied the existing relationship between Bitcoin's trading volume and the number of queries on Google. They reported significant cross correlation values, demonstrating that the volume of searches could predict the trading volume of Bitcoin.

The second group of studies examined Bitcoin's market inefficiencies. Balcilar et al. (2017) discussed the predictability of Bitcoin's returns and volatility based on transaction volume. They found that when extreme events are excluded, volume is an important predictor of price. Urquhart (2017) demonstrated that Bitcoin's price clusters at round numbers. In studying Bitcoin's price dynamics and speculative trading, Blau (2017) concluded that speculative behavior could not be directly linked to the unusual volatility of the Bitcoin market. Brandvold et al. (2015) investigated the role of various Bitcoin exchanges in the price discovery process, noting that the information share is dynamic and evolves significantly over time. Feng et al. (2018) found evidence of informed trading in the Bitcoin market prior to major events. Moreover, they noticed that informed traders prefer to build their positions two days before major positive events and one day before major negative events. This result serves as proof of the market's inefficiency that distinguishes uninformed traders from informed traders of Bitcoin. Finally, Caporale and Plastun (2019) examined the day of the week effect in the cryptocurrency market. They determined that most cryptocurrencies such as Litecoin, Ripple and Dash do not exhibit this anomaly. The only exception is Bitcoin, for which returns on Mondays are significantly higher than those on the other days of the week.

As described above, Bitcoin research concentrates mainly on two factors: the effect of social media on cryptocurrency prices and market anomalies. Using US dollar prices from the beginning of 2012 until the end of March 2020, Cohen (2020) tested whether Darvas Box and linear regression techniques can help traders predict Bitcoin's price trends. Such a long period of time, which includes volatile periods with strong up and down trends, can be challenging for any forecasting system.

3. Data and Methodologies

We investigated whether the ATR, which was originally developed for commodities, could help us make predictions about the pricing trends of five cryptocurrencies. To accomplish this goal, we used the daily price information of three well-established cryptocurrencies (Bitcoin, Ethereum and XRP) from the beginning of 2015 and two more recent cryptocurrencies (Binance Coin and Cardano) from the beginning of 2018. In all cases, we ended with data in the middle of September 2021. We calculated the ATR oscillator using the true range indicator, meaning the greatest of the following: the current high price less the current low price; the absolute value of the current high price less the previous closing price; and the absolute value of the current low price less the previous closing price (Equations 1 and 2). The ATR is thus a moving average, generally using 14 days, of the true ranges.

$$TR_i = \text{Max}\ [(H_i - L_i), (H_i - C_{i-1}), (L_i - C_{i-1})] \tag{1}$$

$$ATR = \left(\frac{1}{n}\right) \sum_{i=1}^{n} TR_i \tag{2}$$

where TRi= a particular true range, H_i = today's highest price, L_i = today's lowest price, C_{i-1} yesterday's closing price, n=the time period employed.

ATR based systems commonly add a multiplier of the ATR (MATR) to the next day's opening price and suggest buying when prices move above that level. Short trades are the opposite: the MATR is subtracted from the opening price and entries occur when that level is broken. The principle of buying and selling according to the ATR system is demonstrated in Figure 1.

Figure 1: ATR Based Trading System

Figure 1 shows the long and short entry points that depend on the ATR and the multiplier of the ATR calculations. The optimization of such a system should adjust the number of days with which the ATR and the MATR are calculated to achieve the best forecasts.

To improve the forecasting capability of our model, we also used the Keltner Channel strategy, first introduced by Chester Keltner in the 1960s. The Keltner Channel is a technical indicator of volatility composed of three separate lines. The original formula used simple moving averages and the high-low price range to calculate the bands. In the 1980s, a new formula was introduced that used the ATR as the measure of volatility. The middle line is the exponential moving average (EMA) of the price. Additional lines are placed above and below the EMA. The upper band is typically set two times the ATR above the EMA, and the lower band is typically set two times the ATR below the EMA. The decision to adopt a long or short position depends on the price breaking the upper band (long) and the lower band (short). Keltner Channels usually use 20-day periods for the oscillator and 10 for the ATR. The calculation is described in Equations 3-5.

$$ML = EMA \tag{3}$$

$$UB = EMA + MATR * ATR \tag{4}$$

$$LB = \text{EMA- MATR}*\text{ATR} \tag{5}$$

where ML= the Keltner Channel's middle line, UB= the Keltner Channel's upper band, LB= the Keltner Channel's lower band, EMA=exponential moving average, and MATR=the ATR's multiplier.

Combining the ATR and the Keltner Channels creates a complex system that demands a powerful optimization system. However, once the system is set up, the trading rules that it generates are quite simple. As Figure 2 illustrates, investors should initiate a long trade when the asset's price bar[2] crosses the upper band and a short trade when the asset's price bar crosses the lower band.

---

[2] A bar is a graphic formation that illustrates the opening, closing, high and low daily prices of assets.

Figure 2: The Keltner Channel Based Trading System

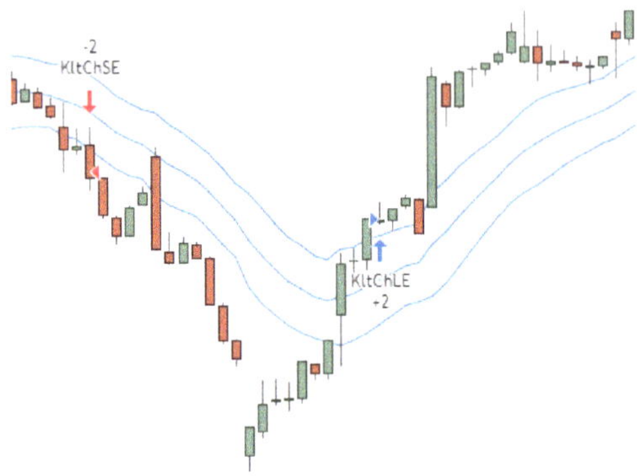

As noted earlier, our algorithmic trading systems are quite complex and require formulas to achieve the best results for multiple objectives. To accomplish this goal, we used particle swarm optimization.

3.1 Particle Swarm Optimization

In many real-life problems, objectives under consideration conflict with each other. Optimizing a solution to achieve one objective can result in unacceptable results with respect to the other objectives. A reasonable solution to a problem with multiple objectives is to investigate a set of solutions, each of which satisfies the objectives at an acceptable level without being dominated by any other solution. Of the various processes developed to achieve these goals, we selected particle swarm optimization developed by Kennedy and Eberhart (1995) (Eberhart et al. 1996). Eberhart and Shi (2001) demonstrated that it could be successfully applied to tracking and optimizing dynamic systems for most optimization problems. However, the most promising applications of this process are in robotics, decision making and simulations, all of which are related to our mission.

Particle swarm optimization uses a stepwise process to change the velocity of each particle toward its best location that maximizes our target function. Next, for each set of particles, we evaluated the desired optimization fitness function using our predefined goals: maximum net profits, the profit factor and the percentage of profitable trades. We then compared the fitness of the setups with "pbest," meaning the setup that achieved the best results in reducing the maximum drawdown and maximizing the percentage of profitable trades, the profit factor, and the net profits. If the current value was better than "pbest," we set the "pbest" value to the current value. In addition, we compared the evaluations of the fitness of the setups with the population's overall previous best. If the current value was better than "gbest," meaning the global best identification, we reset "gbest" to the current value and setups. Finally, we changed the trading setups according to Equation 6 and calculated the results:

$$V (1)\ i+1,d = Vid + C1Rand * Pid - Xid + C2Rand\ Pgd - Xid \quad (1)$$

$$X (2)\ i+1,d = Xid + Vid \quad (2)$$

where Vid = the value of each particle of the setup, Rand = a random number, Pid = the particle's initial identification and Pgd = the particle's global best identification.

We then looped to step 2 (Equation 7) until the largest number of objectives was achieved. The use of a random variable in this process is essential for keeping the optimization process unbiased and to ensure that all variables have an equal chance of entering the process. The random variable represents an initial setup for the trading systems. We created an initial random setup for the trading system and calculated the predefined trading results we sought: the net profit, the profit factor and the percentage of profitable trades. In the next steps, the optimization process altered the setups to achieve better predefined trading results. The particles that were generated for the optimization process were the number of days for the Keltner Channels, the ATR calculation and the MATR. We used this method to optimize the net profits, the profit factor and percentage of profitable trades simultaneously. It also allowed us to train the system and test its performance in a later period.

The net profit is the dollar value of the total net profit generated by the trading system, including a 0.1% trading fee per trade. All trades are executed immediately based on the buy or sell signals generated by the algorithmic trading system. Moreover, the system ignores price slippage and buys at the available price when the system generates a signal (market orders). The profit factor is defined as the gross profits divided by the gross losses. The result indicates the difference between the system's gains and losses. For example, if the profit factor is equal to 1.2, the system generated 20% more profits than losses. The percentage of profitable trades is the percentage of winning trades out of the entire set of trades generated by the system. If it is above 50%, the trading system generated more winning trades than losing trades. However, this does not mean that the net profit of all trades is positive and vice versa. A score less than 50% does not mean that the trading system is losing money. Although one might assume that the three profit indicators move together, in fact they can vary dramatically, and therefore may confuse investors and algorithmic traders. Investors should pick at least one parameter as their target function based on their appetite for risk. For example, more risk averse investors would probably choose to maximize the percentage of profitable trades rather than maximize their net profits. In contrast, investors who are risk seekers are more likely to prefer maximizing their net profits or the profit factor.

Moreover, we also distinguished between long and short positions to examine the ability of the AI to make profitable trades regardless of their length. Thus, we divided the long and short trades for each cryptocurrency using the time frame that maximized the net profit. We compared the results that were generated by our systems to those of a simple buy and hold strategy.

4. Results

Table 1 presents the descriptive statistics and correlation matrix of the daily returns of the five cryptocurrencies. We calculated the results of the buy and hold strategy using the data for each currency. However, the rest of the data in Table 1 are for daily data from the beginning of 2018 until the middle of September 2021.

Table 1: Descriptive Statistics and Correlation Matrix

	Bitcoin	Ethereum	Binance Coin	Cardano	XRP
% DR	0.17	0.25	0.48	0.28	0.15
ST. D	0.040	0.053	0.064	0.064	0.065

Notes: % DR is the average daily return of the buy and hold strategy for Bitcoin, Ethereum and XRP from the beginning of 2015 and for Binance Coin and Cardano from the beginning of 2018. The data of all currencies end in the middle of September 2021. ST. D=standard deviation of the daily returns.

Table 1 shows that the relatively younger currencies, Binance Coin and Cardano, achieved higher average daily returns than the more established currencies of Bitcoin and Ethereum. However, these younger currencies were also more volatile. XRP performed less well than Bitcoin and Ethereum with almost similar volatility as Binance Coin and Cardano.

4.1 Average True Range Trading Results

Table 2 reports the trading results of the ATR based system for Bitcoin and Ethereum using various numbers of days for the ATR calculations and the MATR to generate buy and sell signals. Initially, we considered 14 days for the ATR calculation and 2 for the MATR. We then changed the number of days and the MATR by 0.5 to observe the effect. Tables 2 and 3 show the optimization process and results for the examined cryptocurrencies. Table 4 indicates the results of the long and short trades to optimize the net profits of each cryptocurrency.

Table 2: Trading Results of the ATR Systems for Bitcoin and Ethereum

		Bitcoin			Ethereum		
MATR Days		1.5	2	2.5	1.5	2	2.5
8	NP	49,975	25,313	24,973	4,647	5,049	5,807
	PF	1.84	1.37	1.36	2.36	3.08**	5.11
	PP	43.62	46.47	52.11	46.56	52.81	55.71
9	NP	49,856	31,516	25,824	4,560	4,970	5,743
	PF	1.85	1.48	1.38	2.33	3.06	5.23
	PP	42.86	46.46	52.17	46.56	52.87	55.74**
10	NP	49,507	33,676	26,374	3,704	4,753	5,822
	PF	1.86	1.53	1.39	1.92	2.86	5.33
	PP	41.61	46.32	50.72	45.56	51.69	55.56
11	NP	32,770	50,096**	25,383	3,760	3,920	5,852
	PF	1.47	1.94**	1.37	1.92	2.31	5.3
	PP	41.06	47.31	49.3	45.05	50.55	55.56
12	NP	26,780	48,032	25,445	3,715	3,517	5,857
	PF	1.35	1.87	1.37	1.90	1.99	5.31
	PP	41.5	49.45**	50.72	44.8	49.47	55.56
13	NP	25,027	48,418	25,023	2,381	3,691	5,910
	PF	1.32	1.88	1.38	1.49	2.07	5.36
	PP	42.18	48.39	50.72	44.2	50.54	53.85
14	NP	16,500	48,500	36,552	2,462	3,436	5,969**
	PF	1.19	1.88	1.62	1.52	1.95	5.42**
	PP	42.38	48.39	50.72	43.57	50.52	53.85
15	NP	15,901	48,853	35,566	1,382	4,436	5,913
	PF	1.18	1.83	1.60	1.26	2.57	5.29
	PP	42.48	47.37	50.72	43.06	50.53	53.85
16	NP	15,118	46,645	35,558	1,458	3,628	5,769
	PF	1.17	1.80	1.60	1.28	2.03	5.17
	PP	42.58	48.42	50.72	41.78	48.48	55.38

Notes: NP=Net Profits, PF=Profit Factor, PP=Percentage of Profitable Trades. **= The highest score for each cryptocurrency. MATR=Multiplier of the ATR.

Table 2 indicates that the highest level of net profits of $50,096 and a profit factor of 1.94 were achieved using 11 days for the ATR and 2 for the MATR. In this case, the net profits exceeded those of the buy and hold strategy by $1,795 for the examined period. The best configuration for Ethereum was 14 days for the ATR and 2.5 for the MATR, resulting in $5,969 net profits and a profit factor of 5.42. Moreover, 53.85% of the trades in Ethereum were profitable, indicating that the system involved relatively limited risk. These results demonstrate that the ATR based system can predict the price trends of major two cryptocurrencies.

Our next goal was to optimize the system for Binance Coin, Cardano and XRP. Table 3 presents our results.

Table 3: Trading Results of the ATR Systems for Binance Coin, Cardano and XRP

		Binance Coin			**Cardano**			**XRP**		
MATR Days		1.5	2	2.5	1.5	2	2.5	1.5	2	2.5
8	NP	395.7	530.8	643.4	-0.03	1.71	2.19	-0.11	0.59	1.34
	PF	1.84	2.83	6.07	0.98	2.50	5.17	0.97	1.26	2.17
	PP	30.1	36.07	44.62	38.36	44.44	45.45	33.33	42.22	40.0
9	NP	403.8	530	626.5	-0.35	1.74	2.23	0.00	1.23	1.56**
	PF	1.87	2.83	5.72	0.87	2.55	5.62	1.00	1.71	2.28**
	PP	32.4	36.07	43.59	40.0	44.44	45.45	37	44.2**	40.0
10	NP	253.5	529.1	620.9	-0.68	1.72	2.31**	0.27	0.46	0.36
	PF	1.42	2.82	5.62	0.75	2.53	6.09**	1.1	1.18	1.16
	PP	32.38	36.07	43.59	37.85	42.22	45.6**	38	38.3	37.84
11	NP	236	520.9	664.7	-0.66	1.73	2.30	0.38	0.46	0.38
	PF	1.38	2.77	6.93	0.77	2.54	6.03	1.14	1.18	1.17
	PP	31.78	33.33	48.65	38.96	44.44	41.94	38.36	40.43	37.84
12	NP	35.82	550.7	669**	-0.84	1.64	2.22	0.30	0.54	0.49
	PF	1.04	2.98	7.17**	0.72	2.36	5.19	1.1	1.22	1.24
	PP	31.43	32.84	49.5**	37.66	42.42	41.94	37.33	42.55	37.14
13	NP	25.47	234.7	390.6	-1.66	0.68	2.22	0.73	0.52	0.47
	PF	1.03	1.49	2.09	0.57	1.40	5.13	1.27	1.21	1.23
	PP	30.28	31.88	45.95	35.06	39.22	1.94	39.44	42.55	37.14
14	NP	116.6	298.6	369.2	-1.69	-0.32	2.11	0.76	-0.38	0.49
	PF	1.16	1.67	2.0	0.56	0.88	4.81	1.28	0.86	1.24
	PP	30.84	32.84	45.95	34.18	38.18	42.42	39.44	42.86	37.14
	NP	116.7	304.6	364.6	-2.26	-0.29	2.10	0.75	-0.42	0.64

15	PF	1.16	1.69	1.99	0.47	0.88	4.66	1.28	0.85	1.33
	PP	30.84	34.33	43.59	33.33	38.18	42.42	39.44	42.86	40.0
	NP	130	285.2	370.3	-2.29	-0.25	2.08	-0.21	-0.57	0.46
16	PF	1.18	1.63	2.03	0.47	0.90	4.54	0.94	0.81	1.22
	PP	30.84	35.82	45.95	33.73	38.18	42.42	38.36	43.14	37.14

Notes: NP=Net Profits, PF=Profit Factor, PP=Percentage of Profitable Trades. **= The highest score for each cryptocurrency. MATR=Multiplier of the ATR.

Table 3 shows that the highest net profits for Binance Coin of $669 and a profit factor of 7.17 were achieved using 12 days for the ATR and 2.5 for the MATR. The best configuration for Cardano was 10 days for the ATR and 2.5 for the MATR, resulting in $2.31 net profits and a profit factor of 6.09, which is $0.53 more than the net profits of the buy and hold strategy. The best configuration for XRP was 9 days for the ATR and 2.5 for the MATR, resulting in $1.56 net profits and a profit factor of 2.28.

Figure 2 illustrates the profit factor of our trading system by month from January 2019 through mid-September 2021.

Figure 2: Monthly Profit Factor of the ATR Trading System

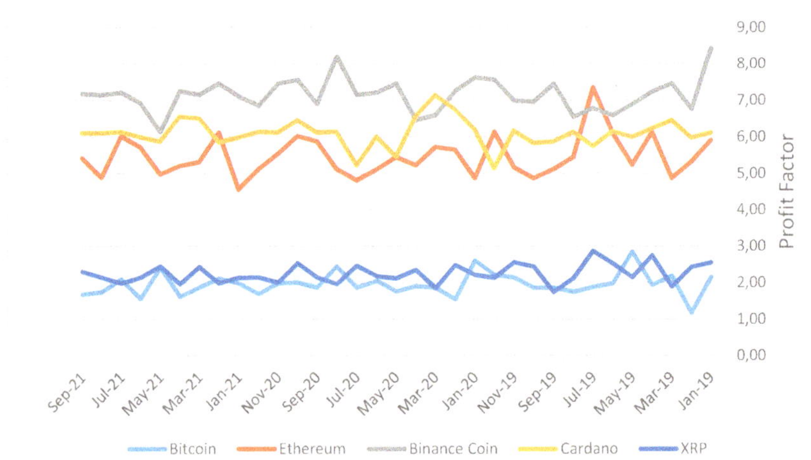

Note: We calculated the monthly profit factor for each cryptocurrency according to its best configuration.

Figure 2 demonstrates that the trading system that is based on the ATR performed better for Binance Coin, Cardano and Ethereum than for Bitcoin and XRP. Furthermore, the dispersion of the profit factor supports the robustness of our system in providing similar results over time.

Table 4 lists the results of the ATR systems for long and short trades.

Table 4: Long and Short Trades for the ATR Systems

Position		Bitcoin	Ethereum	Binance Coin	Cardano	XRP
Long	NP	48,236	4,702	543.1	2.20	1.01
	PF	2.85	23.46	40.89	19.1	2.62
	PP	52.31	69.70	61.11	37.50	33.33
Short	NP	1,860	1,267	125.9	0.11	0.55
	PF	1.01	2.10	2.32	1.32	1.93
	PP	42.19	37.51	35.29	53.33	47.06

Notes: NP=Net Profits, PF=Profit Factor, PP=Percentage of Profitable Trades. The setups are as follows: Bitcoin 11 days and 2 MATR, Ethereum 14 days and 2.5 MATR, Binance Coin 12 days and 2.5 MATR, Cardano 10 days and 2.5 MATR, XRP 9 days and 2.5 MATR.

Table 4 indicates that our ATR based systems are better at forecasting the results of long trades than short trades for all of the examined cryptocurrencies. Moreover, more than 50% of the long trades for Bitcoin, Ethereum and Binance Coin were profitable. In addition, the profit factor for Ethereum and Binance Coin was very high, making the system ideal for long trading those currencies.

4.2 The Keltner Channel Strategy

To add the Keltner Channels to our strategy, we needed to determine an initial number of days for the channels, the ATR and the MATR. We began with 20, 10 and 1, respectively, in accordance with the choices made by many stock traders. We then altered these figures to achieve the highest net profits. As the results in Table 5 indicate, the best results for Bitcoin and Ethereum occurred when the MATR was 1, and the ATR was 9-11 and 14-24.

Table 5: Trading Results of the Keltner Channel Systems for Bitcoin and Ethereum

		Bitcoin			Ethereum		
ATR /Days		9	10	11	9	10	11
14	NP	70,917	68,718	68,026	3,414	3,378	2,878
	PF	4.67	4.69	4.59	4.73	4.62	3.44
	PP	51	53.19	53.19	67.5	67.5	65
15	NP	68,852	70,565	70,565	3,459**	3,419	2,878
	PF	4.91	4.85	4.85	5.08**	4.76	3.44
	PP	53.06	53.19	53.19	71.05**	67.5	65
	NP	69,357	69,357	70,491	3,249	3,208	2,812

16	PF	4.77	4.77	4.84	4.52	4.26	3.38
	PP	54.17	54.17	54.17	62.5	57.14	57.5
	NP	67,608	69,167	69,167	2,332	2,332	2,882
17	PF	4.51	4.76	4.75	3.46	3.46	3.51
	PP	54.17	54.17	54.17	58.54	56.1	57.5
	NP	67,780	67,804	67,698	2,193	2,333	2,442
18	PF	4.53	4.53	4.52	3.26	3.46	3.73
	PP	56.25	56.25	54.17	51.22	56.1	56.41
	NP	83,230**	83,230**	83,230**	2,193	2,303	2,302
19	PF	8.27**	8.27**	8.27**	3.26	3.55	3.55
	PP	56.52**	56.52**	56.52**	51.22	53.85	53.85
	NP	83,041	82,556	81,110	2,347	2,296	2,295
20	PF	8.25	8.19	7.75	3.79	3.54	3.54
	PP	56.52	54.35	52.17	56.76	53.85	53.85
	NP	72,421	81,111	81,111	2,271	2,313	2,075
21	PF	7.03	7.75	7.75	3.65	3.58	2.83
	PP	51.11	52.17	52.17	56.76	53.85	53.85
	NP	71,236	72,538	72,461	2,236	1,956	1,768
22	PF	6.65	7.07	7.04	3.60	2.69	2.53
	PP	51.11	51.11	51.11	56.76	53.85	53.85
	NP	71,468	71,275	71,537	1,808	1,809	1,768
23	PF	6.72	6.66	6.74	2.65	2.65	2.53
	PP	51.11	51.11	51.16	56.76	56.76	53.85
	NP	71,540	71,347	70,844	1,777	1,777	1,889
24	PF	6.74	6.68	6.53	2.59	2.60	2.89
	PP	51.16	51.16	51.16	56.76	56.76	56.76

Notes: NP=Net Profits, PF=Profit Factor, PP=Percent of Profitable Trades. **= The highest score for each cryptocurrency. MATR=Multiplier of the ATR.

As the table indicates, the trading results using the Keltner Channels with the best configuration improved those of the stand-alone ATR system dramatically. The system best setup for Bitcoin achieved a net profit of $83,230 compared to the $50,096 of the ATR system. The Keltner Channel based system also produced positive returns for Ethereum. However, its net profit of $3,459 was less than the $5,969 that the stand-alone ATR system produced. It is important to add that the best Ethereum results were achieved with a 5.08 profit factor. In addition, 71.05% of its trades were profitable.

Table 6 presents the results of the best configurations of the trading systems for Binance Coin, Cardano and XRP.

Table 6: Trading Results of the Keltner Channel Systems for Binance Coin, Cardano and XRP

		Binance Coin			Cardano			XRP		
ATR /Days		9	10	11	2	3	4	2	3	4
14	NP	674.4	673.4	618.9	1.76	1.57	2.43	1.65	2.64**	1.73
	PF	19.27	19	17.54	4.05	3.71	17.06	1.88	2.90**	2.41
	PP	56	56	54.17	46.15	45.15	50	44.44	40.23	42.7
15	NP	674.8	674	618.5	1.75	1.53	2.37	1.61	2.62	2.08
	PF	19.28	19.26	17.53	4.01	3.65	16.32	1.85	2.82	2.71
	PP	56	56	54.17	46.15	46.15	50	43.04	42.17	43.9
16	NP	679.4	673.8	673.8	2.49	2.36	2.38	2.12	1.94	2.26
	PF	20.75	19.26	19.26	15.23	15.47	16.43	2.30	2.33	2.78
	PP	56	56	56	50	50	50	42.86	43.21	44.44
17	NP	679.2	674	673.8	2.51**	2.38	2.36	2.06	1.82	2.09
	PF	20.74	19.2	19.26	17.92**	17.88	15.47	2.26	2.18	2.51
	PP	56	56	56	54.55**	54.55	50	42.67	41.98	44.16
18	NP	674.6	673.4	669.4	2.50	2.39	2.36	2.16	1.58	1.96
	PF	19.38	19	18	16.82	18.43	15.47	2.37	1.95	2.32
	PP	56	56	56	54.55	54.55	50	41.33	41.77	43.04
19	NP	674.8	673.6	669.6	2.38	2.40	2.40	1.79	1.26	1.85
	PF	19.43	19.1	18.1	16.05	18.87	19.17	2.24	1.68	2.18
	PP	56	56	56	54.55	54.55	54.55	42.25	37.97	41.98
20	NP	674.8	673.6	675	2.38	2.36	2.39	1.61	1.72	2.11
	PF	19.43	19.1	20.23	15.84	16.52	18.43	2.0	2.1	2.46
	PP	56	56	60	54.55	54.55	54.55	42.25	38.67	40.51
	NP	669.8	673.8	673	2.38	2.35	2.35	1.75	1.65	1.61

21	PF	18.95	20.7	19.6	15.84	16.29	16.29	2.27	2.10	1.98
	PP	56	60	60	54.55	54.55	54.55	43.28	38.36	38.67
22	NP	669.6	674.2	669.8	2.38	2.35	2.35	1.74	1.59	1.65
	PF	18.95	20.88	19.55	15.84	16.29	16.29	2.56	2.04	2.05
	PP	56	60	60	54.55	54.55	54.54	44.62	39.44	39.44
23	NP	676	666.2	669.8	2.32	2.35	2.35	1.75	1.67	1.55
	PF	22.87	19.6	19.55	15.5	16.29	16.29	2.26	2.16	2.03
	PP	60	60	60	54.55	54.55	54.54	44.44	43.08	40.58
24	NP	676	680.2	680.2	2.32	2.35	2.35	1.69	1.59	1.48
	PF	22.87	28.1	28.1	15.20	16.29	16.29	2.17	2.10	1.97
	PP	60	65.22	65.22	54.55	54.55	54.54	44.44	43.08	40.58
25	NP	680.4	684.8	684.8	2.32	2.36	2.35	1.67	1.59	1.62
	PF	25.65	32.41	32.41	15.22	16.31	15.98	2.16	2.10	2.16
	PP	65.22	71.43	71.43	54.55	54.55	54.55	45.9**	43.08	43.08
26	NP	278	698**	698**	2.32	2.34	2.35	1.70	1.59	1.09
	PF	4.44	32.87**	32.87**	15.22	16.16	15.98	2.19	2.10	1.63
	PP	66.67	71.43**	71.43**	54.55	54.55	54.55	45.9**	43.08	41.54

Notes: NP=Net Profits, PF=Profit Factor, PP=Percent of Profitable Trades. **= The highest score for each cryptocurrency. MATR=Multiplier of the ATR.

As the table indicates, the best setup for Binance Coin is 26 days for the Keltner Channels formation with 10 or 11 days for the ATR calculation. That configuration resulted in $698 net profits, with a 32.87 profit factor and 71.43% profitable trades. Moreover, adding the Keltner Channel system also improved the results of the stand-alone ATR system for Binance Coin by $29 and produced a much better profit factor and many more profitable trades. Cardano's best results were achieved using 17 days for the Keltner Channels and 2 days for the ATR. This setup produced $2.51 in net profits, $0.20 above the ATR stand-alone system. It also resulted in a 17.92 profit factor and 54.55% profitable trades. XRP's best results were achieved using 14 days for the Keltner Channels and 3 days for the ATR. This setup produced $2.64 in net profits, $1.08 above the ATR stand-alone system. It also resulted in a 2.9 profit factor.

Figure 3 illustrates the profit factor of the Keltner Channel trading system by month.

Figure 3: Monthly Profit Factor of the Keltner Channels Trading System

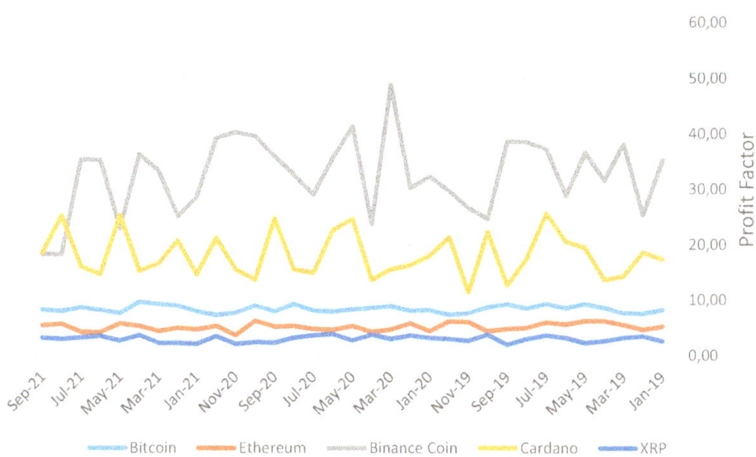

The figure indicates that Binance Coin and Cardano have a higher profit factor but more volatility than Bitcoin, Ethereum and XRP.

Table 7 lists the results of the Keltner Channel systems for long and short trades.

Table 7: Long and Short Positions for the Keltner Channels Algorithmic Trading

Position		Bitcoin	Ethereum	Binance Coin	Cardano	XRP
Long	NP	63,567	3,302	544	2.29	1.83
	PF	12.96	16	58.3	25.1	3.60
	PP	69.57	78.95	90.91	45.45	38.64
Short	NP	19,663	157	154	0.22	0.81
	PF	4.20	1.25	8.61	5.1	2.18
	PP	43.48	63.16	50	63.64	41.86

Notes: NP=Net Profits, PF=Profit Factor, PP=Percent of Profitable Trades. The number of days for the Keltner Channels and the ATR are as follows: Bitcoin 19 and 10, Ethereum 15 and 9, Binance Coin 26 and 10, Cardano 17 and 2, XRP 14 and 3.

Table 7 demonstrates that like the ATR systems, the Keltner Channel systems perform better for long trades than for short trades for all of the examined currencies.

5. Conclusions and Implications

This research is an initial attempt to design, optimize and use ATR based trading systems for popular cryptocurrencies. We assessed the optimal system in terms of its ability to maximize net profits, the profit factor and the percentage of profitable trades. We established that ATR based systems can predict the price trends of both well-established and newly created cryptocurrencies. We also demonstrated that adding optimized Keltner Channel based systems improved the forecasting ability of the stand-alone optimized ATR systems and produced better results in terms of net profits and profit factors. Finally, both systems performed better for long trades than for short trades. Our results should prove helpful to investors trying to forecast the price trends of the major cryptocurrencies.

Data Availability: The data can be obtained upon request

References

Baek, C., Elbeck, M. (2014). Bitcoin as an investment or speculative vehicle? A first look. Applied Economics Letters, 22, 30–34.

Balcilar, M., Bouri, E., Gupta, R., et al. (2017). Can volume predict Bitcoin returns and volatility? A quantiles-based approach. Economic Modelling, 64, 74–81.

Blau, B. M. (2017). Price dynamics and speculative trading in Bitcoin. Research in Business Finance, 41, 493–499.

Brandvold, M., Molner, P., Vagstad, K., et al. (2015). Price discovery on Bitcoin exchanges. Journal of international Finance Markets Institutions and Money, 36, 18–35.

Caporale, M. G., Plastun, A. (2019). The day of the week effect in the cryptocurrency market, Finance Research Letters, 31, 258–269.

Chow, Y. S., Robbins, H., Siegmund, D. (1971). Great expectations: The theory of optimal stopping. Boston, MA: Houghton Mifflin.

Cohen, G. (2020). "Forecasting Bitcoin Trends Using Algorithmic Learning Systems", Entropy-MDPI, *22*(8), 838.

Eberhart, R. C., & Shi, Y. (2001). Tracking and optimizing dynamic systems with particle swarms. Seoul: Congress on Evolutionary Computation.

Eberhart, R. C., Simpson, P. K., & Dobbins, R. W. (1996). Computational intelligence PC tools. Boston: Academic Press Professional.

Feng, W., Wang, Y., Zang, Z. (2018). Informed trading in the Bitcoin market. Finance Research Letters, 26, 63–70.

Garcia, D., Schweizer, F. (2015). Social signals and algorithmic trading of Bitcoin. R Soc Open Sci, 2, 9.

Kennedy, J., & Eberhart, R. C. (1995). Practical Swarm Optimization. In International conference on neural networks, IV, 1942–1948.

Kim, Y. B., Kim, J. G., Kim, W., Im, J. H., Kim, T. H., Kang, S. J., et al. (2016). Predicting fluctuations in cryptocurrency transactions based on user comments and replies. PLoS ONE, 11, 8.

Liu, Y., Yang, A., Zhang, J., & Jingjing, Y. (2020). An optimal stopping problem of detecting entry points for trading modeled by geometric Brownian motion. Computational Economics, 55, 827–843.

Matta, M., Lunesu, L., & Marchesi, M. (2015). The predictor impact of Web search media on Bitcoin trading volumes. In 7th International Joint Conference On Knowledge Discovery, Knowledge Engineering And Knowledge Management.

Moore, T., & Christin, N. (2013). Beware the middleman: Empirical analysis of Bitcoin-exchange risk.In A. R. Sadeghi (Ed.), Financial cryptography and data security. FC 2013. Lecture Notes in Computer Science (Vol. 7859). Berlin: Springer.

Urquhart, A. (2017). Price clustering in Bitcoin. Economics Letters, 159, 145mics

Wilder, J.W. (1978). New concept of Technical

Forecasting Gold Price Using Machine Learning Methodologies

Cohen Gil and Aiche Avishay *

Abstract

This study investigates the potential of advanced Machine Learning (ML) methodologies to predict fluctuations in the price of gold. The study employs data from leading global stock indices, the S&P500 VIX volatility index, major commodity futures, and 10-year bond yields from the US, Germany, France, and Japan. Lagged values of these features up to 10 previous days are also used. Four machine learning models are used: Random Forest, Gradient Boosted Regression Trees (GBRT), and Extreme Gradient Boosting (XGBoost), to forecast future gold prices. The study finds that the most influential stocks indices for prediction are one-day lagged data of ASX, S&P500, TA35, IBEX, and AEX, as well as U.S. and Japan bonds yields and delayed data of gas and silver. Furthermore, the study's models identify that one-day lagged VIX score and our VIX dummy variable have a significant impact on gold price, indicating that economic uncertainty affects gold prices. The results suggest that incorporating various financial indicators and moving averages can be a powerful tool for predicting future gold prices. GBRT and XGBoost can be valuable models for making informed decisions about gold investments.

Keywords: Commodities, Machine Learning, Regression Trees, Gradient Boosted Regression Trees, Extreme Gradient Boosting.

* Cohen Gil and Aiche Avishay are from the Management Department, Western Galilee Academic College, Acre, Israel

1. Introduction

Gold is known to serve as a hedging commodity against stock crashes and high inflation (see for example Adekoya et al. [1]). Gold is also known to serve as a "safe haven" against stock market crashes and economic uncertainty. Researchers have examined, for example, the role of gold in the Covid-19 pandemic and found that investors expanded investment in gold during the crisis (Akhtaruzzman et al. [2], Wen et al. [3]). Wang and Lee [4] tested whether gold is a" safe haven "for exchange rate risks of five major world currencies and concluded that gold could act as a" safe haven "to hedge dynamic risk for the euro, dollar, and pound in the short run, but not for the renminbi and yen. This important role of gold as a" safe haven "commodity for different financial markets crises stresses the need for a reliable forecasting methodology that would enable portfolio managers, hedgers, and financial institutions to combine gold effectively in their portfolios.

Economic uncertainty usually increases the financial markets fear which is commonly measured by the VIX implied stock market volatility index. Prior research has tried to explain the roll of Gold, Bitcoin, and the U.S VIX as hedging tools against economic uncertainty. Shahzad et al. [5] compared the hedging abilities of those assets against the downside movements of the BRICS countries stock market indices and concluded that the Bitcoin and Gold are weak hedges. However, their results show that Gold appears to a higher and more stable diversification benefits in China while the VIX exhibits higher diversification benefits in, Russia, Brazil, India, and South Africa. Fakhfekh et al. [6] found that both Bitcoin and Gold have remarkable hedging abilities. Their results show that the VIX is the most effective instrument for hedging stock market indices. Elsayed at al. [7] studied the dynamic connectedness of return and volatility spillovers among cryptocurrency, Gold, and uncertainty measures. They found that Gold is the net receiver of both the return and the volatility spillovers under all market conditions.

Until recently, researchers have used traditional econometrics to predict gold prices using predetermined hypotheses concerning the correlations between gold and other financial assets. However ,these methodologies have been upgraded since Artificial Intelligence (AI) and Machine Learning (ML) capabilities have been developed. Those methodologies have produced a revolution in financial assets price forecasting precision far better than ever been achieved before.

Moreover, this new approach to research, have is able to identify nonlinear and complex dependencies that cannot be observed by other methods. In the following research we used the following research ML capabilities to explore interdependencies among multiple financial markets to predict gold prices. Our data contains the world's leading stock indices of all 38 OECD countries, commodities futures, leading 10 years' Bonds yields along with the VIX volatility. The uniqueness of the following research is that it tries to predict gold price volatility using a data set that covers three financial markets: Stocks, Commodities, and Bonds. Prior research has concentrated on the link between gold prices and other commodities, others have investigated the correlation between gold price and stocks indices. However, non, have included bond yields predictors that serve as an alternative "safe haven" to gold and such a variety of world's leading stocks indices. Such a data scope enables us to evaluate the relative influence of the OECD countries financial data on gold prices. In addition to the use of the raw data, lagged and Moving Averages (MA) are also being used to identify trends and correlations more easily. These three layers of data (raw, lagged, and MA) provide much more information than the raw data itself that was used in prior research.

This study employs advanced machine learning techniques such as Random Forest, Gradient Boosted Regression Trees (GBRT), and Extreme Gradient Boosting (XGBoost) which have demonstrated efficacy in predicting other financial assets. The efficiency of the Random Forest, GBRT, and XGBoost models in predicting gold price fluctuations can be attributed to their ability to capture non-linear relationships between explanatory variables and the target variable. In addition, the models have the capability to handle large datasets with multiple features and can effectively handle missing or incomplete data. Moreover, the models can be optimized through cross-validation and grid search techniques to select the best hyperparameters, thus improving their accuracy. The results of our study have shown that these models were able to accurately predict gold price fluctuations, with the XGBoost model achieving the highest level of accuracy. Furthermore, in order to identify the most relevant variables among a large set of potential predictors, we implemented stepwise selection to reduce the number of predictors of gold price. Additionally, to explore deep and remote dependencies, we used up to 10th order of lagged data of each variable including gold itself. The combination of these methods allowed us to efficiently identify the most influential factors in predicting gold price fluctuations.

We found that the most influential stocks indices are found to be one-day lagged data of ASX, S&P500, TA35, IBEX, and AEX, U.S., and Japan bonds yields, and delayed data of gas and silver. Moreover, the VIX score has an important impact on gold prices suggesting, that economic uncertainty influences gold prices. Moreover, this study identified that GBRT and XGBoost could be useful models for gold price forecasting enabling decision-makers to make informed decisions about combining gold in their portfolios.

2. Literature Review

Precious metals price volatility has been a puzzle that many researchers have tried to solve. Zheng [5] explained that precious metal futures have higher returns when investor sentiment is pessimistic rather than optimistic. Bosch and Pradkhan [6] argued that changes in traders' positions have a destabilizing impact on subsequent conditional volatility in gold, silver, and palladium. Qadan [7] claimed that investors' risk appetite and economic uncertainty are driving precious metal price and their volatility. Rehman et al. [8] have identified the safe-haven nature of precious metals against an oil price drop. Other researchers have explored the link between previous metals to other commodities. Wang and Li [9] offered a predictive model of the prices of three commodities: Oil, Corn, and Gold. They used various scales within a singular spectrum analysis to identify causalities between those future markets. Kang [10] examined spillover effects among six commodity futures markets and found that gold and silver are information transmitters to other commodity futures markets.

Since financial markets are characterized by high complexity and volatility researchers are using Support Vector Machines (SVM) systems for price forecasting and portfolio optimizations. The SVM allows errors within the training data resulting in a significantly reduced error in the test data. Another technique that is used to forecasts the price volatility of financial assets is Long Short-Term Memory (LSTM). This methodology contains three main stages, input, forget, and output which controls the flow of information over time. The forget gate allows the system to decide which data is not relevant to financial forecasting and therefore should be ignored. Akyildirim et al. [11] analyzed the predictive power of the SVM model for cryptocurrencies and argued that at daily or minute levels, the SVM classification algorithms reached about 55–65% of predictive accuracy. Chen et al. [12] used the LSTM model to predict the direction of Chinese stocks and showed a 13% forecasting improvement compared to other methods. Borovkova and Tsiamas [13] offered an LSTM model for intraday stock predictions based on technical analysis indicators and found that their model performed better than equally weighted ensembles or benchmark models. Fischer and Krauss [14] used the LSTM system to predict the S&P500 index and reported that this type of forecasting methodology is superior to other ML methods and traditional trading strategies.

Several studies have utilized ML methodologies to try to forecast gold prices. Plakandaras and Ji [15], used an algorithm based on the Support Vector Regression (SVR) for gold forecasting. Their findings show a significant increase in returns generated by the trading strategy .Zhang and Ci [16] used a deep belief network model composed of restricted Boltzmann machines for gold price forecasting .Their results show that the model improved accuracy for gold price forecasting compared to the traditional neural network and linear models. Vidal and Kristjanpoller [17] attempted to forecast gold volatility by combining two deep learning methodologies: LSTM added to convolutional neural networks. They documented a substantial improvement compared to the GARCH and LSTM models .Alameer et al. [18] proposed a model that combines the adaptive neuro-fuzzy inference system and genetic algorithm that can forecast copper prices .Their model improved the forecasting accuracy and decrease the mean square error of traditional models . Livieris et al. [19] proposed a deep learning forecasting model for gold price exploiting the ability of convolutional layers along with LSTM layers and concluded that their model could provide a significant boost to forecasting performance. Jianwei et al. [20] combined Independent Component Analysis (ICA) and Gate Recurrent Neural Network (GRUNN) methods to forecast gold prices and concluded that the fluctuation of the gold price will be interrupted by long-term trends, cyclic recurrent factors, and random events. Moreover, their ICA-GRUNN model provides prediction with high accuracy and outperforms benchmark methods. He et al. [21] proposed gold price forecasting using an integration of LSTM and Convolutional Neural Networks (CNN). Their model that enables to capture of the local patterns and abstracting the spatial features outperformed other conventional forecasting methods.

3. Data and Methodologies

Our analysis aims to predict the daily price change of gold price using data of major commodities futures, world leading indices, and U.S, Germany, France, and Japan, 10 years bonds yields. The commodities futures are gold, silver, oil, natural gas, and wheat. These commodities represent four commodities major sectors, energy, precious metal, energy, and food. The world-leading stocks indices included all 38 OECD countries as primary data for global stock volatilities. Additionally, we included the VIX volatility indices to provide a measure of market uncertainty. The VIX was used both as a continuous variable and as a dummy variable in which above 20 represents extreme market volatility and below 20 normal market condition. Our data consists of daily prices of the above assets from February 2011 to February 2023. We then split the data into train and test sets on September 26, 2019. For the predictions, we applied four machine learning (ML) methodologies: Four machine learning models are used: Random Forest, Gradient Boosted Regression Trees (GBRT), and Extreme Gradient Boosting (XGBoost), to forecast future gold prices. To conduct our analysis, we took the first differences of each series including the gold itself, and generated lagged series of the first, second, third, and up to the 10th order, resulting in a dataset with 276 features. Furthermore, we also calculated the Moving Averages (MA) of the time series, which is a known technical analysis enabling us to identify market trends more easily than the raw data itself. A full list of the selected explanatory variables is presented in Appendix 1.

3.1 Regression Tree (RT)

A regression tree is a type of decision tree used in machine learning for predicting a continuous target variable based on several input features. It uses a tree-like model of decisions and possible consequences, specifically target predictions, to go from observations about an item to conclusions about the item's target value. The internal nodes of the tree represent test conditions on features, each branch represents the outcome of the test, and each leaf node represents a prediction for the target value. Yu et al. [22], for example, used various ML methods and found that classification RT can predict accurately credit rating for different debt grades such as speculative, investment, and default. RT is usually used when the tree has many leaves features that interact in a nonlinear complicated way. Moreover, the tree feature presents a recursive partition consisting of terminal nodes. RT formulation is described in Equation 1 and the sum of square errors for tree T in Equation 2.

$$Y = \beta_0 + \beta^T X + \gamma X X^T + \epsilon \tag{1}$$

$$S = \sum_{c \in leaves\ (T)} \sum_{i \in c} (y_i - m_c)^2 \tag{2}$$

Where: $m_c = \frac{1}{n_c} \sum_{i \in c} y_i$ is the predictor of leaf c.

3.2 Random Forest (RF)

RF regression is an ensemble machine-learning technique for regression problems. It combines multiple decision trees into a single model, where each tree is trained on a random subset of the data and features. The final prediction is made by averaging the predictions of individual trees. The idea behind this approach is that by combining the predictions of multiple trees, the model reduces overfitting and improves the accuracy of the predictions. The random selection of features in each tree also adds to the diversity of the trees and reduces the correlation between them, further improving the overall performance of the model. Ghosh et al. [23], for example, used LSTM networks and RF procedures to forecast the movement of the S&P500 and concluded that their multi-feature setting provided a daily return of 0.64%. Derbenstev et al. [24] applied RF and Gradient Boosting Machine (GBM) to forecast major cryptocurrency prices and concluded that using ML methodologies can forecast short-term cryptocurrency prices and can be the basis for automated trading systems. For output the ensemble of trees $\{T_b\}_1^B$, the regression function is the follows:

$$\hat{f}_{rf}^B(x) = \frac{1}{B} \sum_{b=1}^{B} T_b(X) \tag{3}$$

If the variables are identically distributed with a positive pairwise correlations ρ , the variance can be expressed as:

$$V = \rho\sigma^2 + \frac{1-\rho}{B}\sigma^2 \tag{4}$$

After B trees are grown $\{T(X;\theta_b)\}_1^B$, The RF regression predictor is defined as:

$$\hat{f}_{rf}^{B}(x) = \frac{1}{B}\sum_{b=1}^{B} T_b(x;\ \theta_b) \quad (5)$$

3.3 Gradient Boosted Regression Trees (GBRT)

Gradient Boosting is an ensemble learning method that combines multiple weak prediction models into a single strong model. In the case of regression, the weak models are typically decision trees, and the combination of multiple decision trees is called a Gradient Boosted Regression Tree (GBRT) model.

At a high level, gradient boosting works by iteratively training a sequence of decision trees on the residuals of the previous trees. In each iteration, the algorithm adds a new tree to the sequence that tries to predict the remaining errors that were not explained by the previous trees. The final prediction is the sum of the predictions of all the trees in the sequence. If we denote $T_i(x)$ to be the prediction function of the i decision tree in the sequence of K trees then the final prediction function may be written as

$$f(x) = \sum_{i=1}^{K} T_i(x) \quad (6)$$

Each decision tree in the sequence is trained to predict the negative gradient of the loss function with respect to the current model's predictions. The loss function used in regression problems is usually the mean squared error (MSE) which measures the difference between the predicted and actual values. The loss function for the i-th iteration can be written as:

$$L_i = \sum_{i=1}^{K} l(y_i, f_{i-1}(x_i) + T_i(x_i) \quad (7)$$

where L_i is the loss function for the i-th iteration, y_i is the actual value of the target variable for the i-th data point, $f_{i-1}(x_i)$ is the predicted value of the target variable by the model in the $(i-1)$-th iteration, $T_i(x_i)$ is the prediction of the i-th decision tree for the input x_i, and $l(\cdot)$ is the loss function for a single data point, which is usually MSE.

The algorithm then tries to minimize the loss function L_i by adjusting the parameters of the decision tree, such as the split points and the leaf values. Once the i-th decision tree is trained, its prediction is added to the previous trees' predictions, and the process is repeated for the $(i+1)$-th iteration until a stopping criterion is met.

3.4 Extreme Gradient Boosting (XGBoost)

Extreme Gradient Boosting (XGBoost) is a powerful machine learning algorithm used for regression and classification problems. It is an implementation of gradient boosted decision trees designed to optimize both computational efficiency and predictive accuracy.

XGBoost works by creating an ensemble of weak prediction models, in this case, decision trees, and iteratively improving their predictions by minimizing a loss function. It does so by using gradient descent optimization on the loss function.

XGBoost regression model can be broken down into the following components:

The objective function minimizes the difference between predicted and actual values. The objective function can be written as:

$$L(\hat{y}, y) = \sum_i l(\hat{y}_i, y_i) + \sum_k \Omega(f_k) \tag{10}$$

where $\hat{y}$ is the predicted value, y is the true value, $l(\cdot)$ is the loss function that measures the difference between predicted and true values, f_k is the k-th decision tree, and $\Omega(f_k)$ is the regularization term that penalizes the complexity of the model.

XGBoost builds an ensemble of decision trees by iteratively improving the predictions of the previous trees. Each subsequent tree is built to correct the errors of the previous tree. This process is called gradient boosting. Specifically, the objective function of the next tree is designed to minimize the residual error of the previous tree.

To avoid overfitting, XGBoost adds regularization to the objective function. The regularization term includes two components: the first is the L1 regularization term (Lasso regularization) which adds the absolute value of the weights of the decision tree to the objective function. The second is the L2 regularization term (Ridge regularization), which adds the square of the weights of the decision tree to the objective function. These regularization terms help to prevent overfitting and improve the generalization ability of the model.

XGBoost uses the CART algorithm to construct decision trees. At each node, it evaluates all possible splits and selects the one that leads to the largest reduction in the objective function. It then prunes the tree using a second-order Taylor approximation to the objective function to improve computational efficiency.

The final prediction of the XGBoost model is the sum of the predictions of all the decision trees in the ensemble, weighted by the learning rate (a hyperparameter that controls the contribution of each tree).

4. Results

4.1 Regression tree

In order to predict fluctuations in gold prices, a regression tree analysis was conducted. This type of analysis is used to model the relationship between a dependent variable and one or more independent variables. The pruned tree in Figure 1 represents the variables and values that resulted in the best predictive performance based on cross-validation. By pruning the tree, the model is optimized to avoid overfitting, which is a common issue with decision tree models. Compared to linear regression models, the regression tree model can identify complex, non-linear relationships between variables. As a result, it provides a useful tool for forecasting gold fluctuations. The pruned tree presented in Figure 2 offers valuable insights into the most important variables and their relationships, making it a valuable resource for understanding the factors that affect gold prices.

Figure 1: Optimization to Prune the Regression Tree

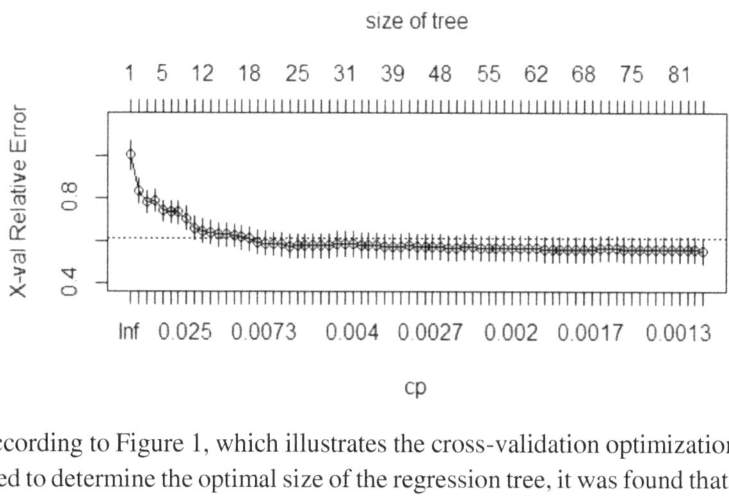

According to Figure 1, which illustrates the cross-validation optimization process used to determine the optimal size of the regression tree, it was found that a pruned tree with 17 final leaves would provide the best forecast. The plot in Figure 1 provides a visual representation of the trade-off between model complexity and predictive accuracy, allowing for the selection of the most appropriate tree size. Ultimately, the decision to use a pruned tree with 17 final leaves will allow for the most accurate and effective forecasting of gold fluctuations.

Figure 2: The Pruned Regression Tree

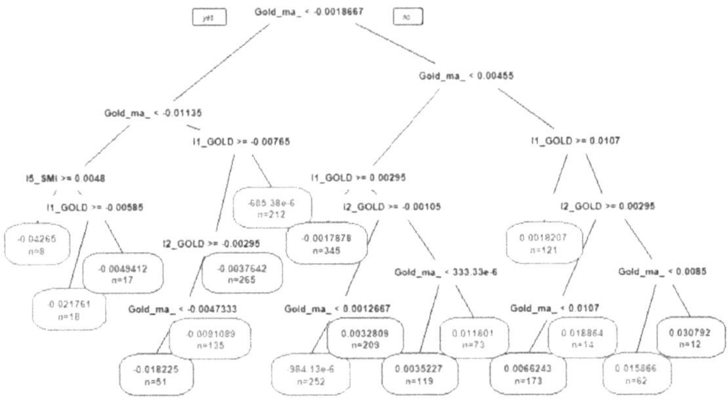

According to the cross-validation pruning shown in Figure 2, a pruned tree with 17 final leaves was found to produce the best forecast for gold fluctuations. The decision tree algorithm selected the variables of 3 and 5 days moving averages, one and two days lag gold fluctuations, and five days-lagged SMI as they were the most significant in predicting fluctuations in gold prices. These variables allowed the model to capture both the overall trend of the commodity and the influence of past fluctuations on the current fluctuations. The relative test means squared error (RSE) of 0.6401 and test mean squared error (MSE) of 0.000071772 suggest that the model performed well in predicting the target variable in previously unseen data, indicating good generalization performance and accuracy. In Figure 3, the scatterplot illustrates the relationship between the actual fluctuations of gold prices and the predicted values from the regression tree model. The plot shows that the predicted values are in agreement with the actual values, as indicated by the red line representing the 45-degree line starting from the origin.

Figure 3: Scatterplot of Real vs. Predicted Gold Fluctuations

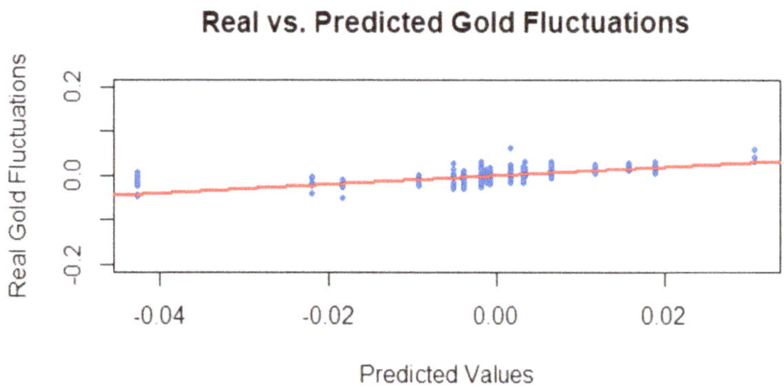

4.2 Random Forest

Random Forest (RF) is an ensemble method that combines multiple decision trees to improve the accuracy and robustness of the model. Figure 4 illustrates the relationship between the mean squared error (MSE) and the number of trees used in the random forest process. As the number of trees increases, the MSE generally decreases, but there comes a point where adding more trees does not significantly improve the performance. In this case, the plot shows that the MSE reaches a plateau after 30 trees. However, the minimum MSE is attained at 463 trees, hence, this is the number of trees that are ultimately used for the analysis (see Figure 4).

Figure 4: The Optimal Number of Trees in the RF Process

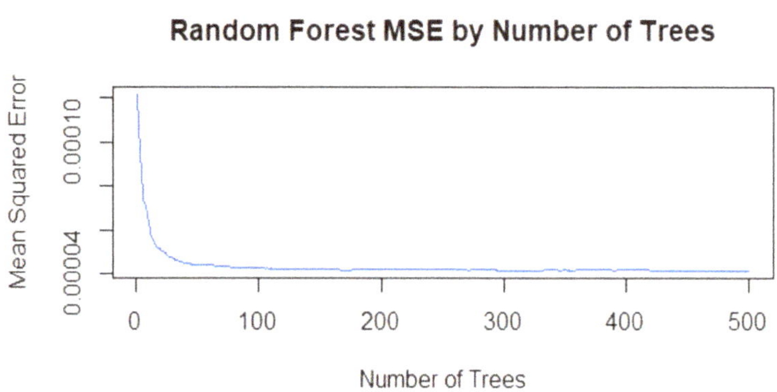

The RF model was employed to forecast gold fluctuations, and the results show that it had moderate accuracy in predicting future gold price movements. The model generated a test relative mean squared error (RSE) of 0.43635 and a test MSE of 0.00004892, indicating a performance improvement compared to the regression tree model. The RSE value of 0.43635 indicates that the model's predictions were relatively close to the actual values, and the test MSE value of 0.00004892 shows that the model's predictions were accurate. Additionally, it's worth mentioning that the random forest model provides information about the importance of each input variable in predicting gold fluctuations. This information can be used to gain insights into the factors that have the greatest influence on gold prices and can guide investment decisions accordingly. Moreover, the model can be continually updated and refined as new data becomes available, allowing for improved predictions over time. Overall, the random forest model proved to be a useful tool in forecasting gold price fluctuations, and the improved RSE value suggests that this model was better suited for this task compared to the regression tree model.

The relationship between the random forest predictions and the actual gold fluctuations is illustrated in Figure 5, where a 45-degree line is included to emphasize the strength of the relationship between the two variables. The scatter plot reveals a high correlation between the predicted values from the random forest model and the actual gold fluctuations, with most of the data points lying relatively close to the 45-degree line. This visual evidence supports the model's accuracy in predicting gold price movements and suggests that it can be a valuable tool for making informed decisions about gold investments.

Figure 5: Scatterplot of real vs. predicted Gold fluctuations

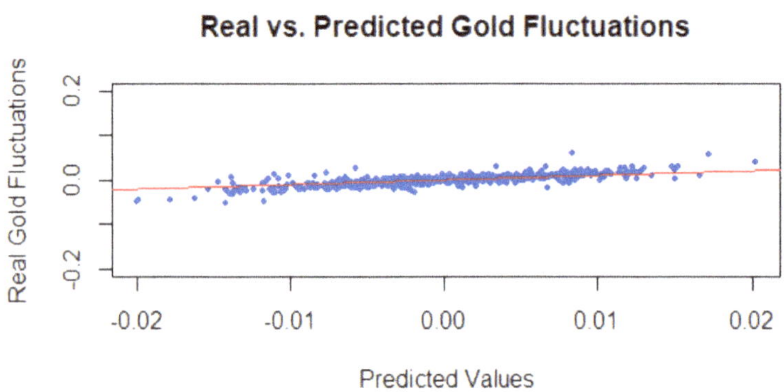

The RF methodology identifies the contribution of each explanatory variable to the accuracy of the random forest model (for the full list see Appendix 2). The model identifies that gold 3 days Moving Average (MA) has the highest contribution to the current daily gold price movement followed by lagged data of gold from 1-4 prior days. The most influential stock indices are found to be one-day lagged data of ASX, S&P500, TA35, IBEX, and AEX. Out of the four countries' 10 years bond yields, (US, Germany, France, and Japan) only U.S. and Japan bond yields contributed information to gold price forecasting. The most influential other commodities on gold prices are delayed data of gas and silver (prior 6 and 8 days, respectively). The model has also identified that one-day lagged VIX score and our VIX dummy variable have an important impact on gold price suggesting, that economic uncertainty influences gold prices.

4.3 Gradient Boosted Regression Tree (GBRT)

Gradient Boosting is an ensemble learning method that combines multiple decision trees into a single strong model. In this study, we used a five-fold cross-validation technique to optimize for the number of trees and the maximum depth of each tree. Figure 6 exhibits the outcomes of our cross-validation study, indicating that the minimum cross-validation means squared error (MSE) is obtained at 1100 iterations. We selected a maximum tree depth of 15, which was established through grid search as the optimal configuration for our GBRT model. With this optimal configuration, our GBRT model achieved a test MSE of 0.000018605 and a relative MSE of 0.16593, suggesting a significant improvement compared to the random forest model. These values indicate that our model had a high degree of accuracy in predicting future gold price movements.

Figure 6: Optimization for the Number of Iterations in GBRT

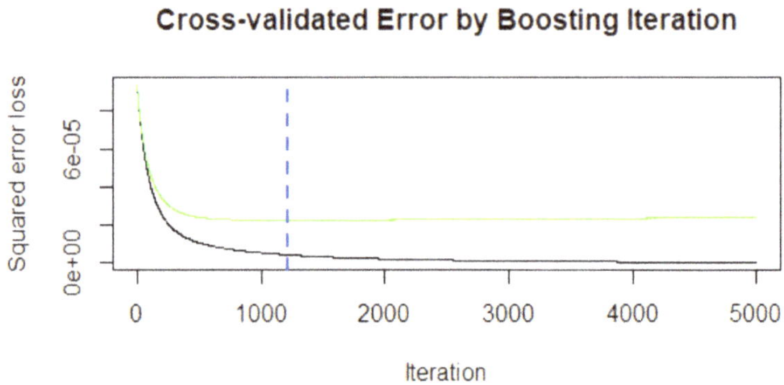

Figure 7 displays the relationship between the predicted values from our GBRT model and the actual gold price movements. The plot shows that there is a low variance of distribution around the 45-degree line, indicating that the predicted values closely match the actual values. The scatter plot illustrates that most of the predicted values from our GBRT model fall close to the 45-degree line, suggesting that the model's predictions were highly accurate for a large number of data points.

Figure 7: Scatterplot of Real vs. Predicted Gold Fluctuations

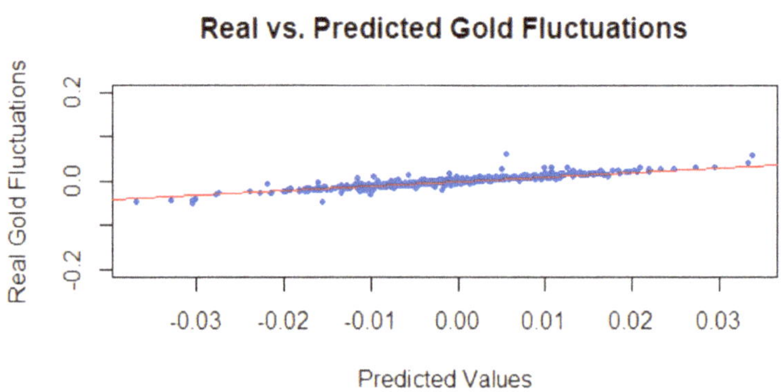

4.5 Extreme Gradient Boost (XGBoost)

The XGBoost algorithm is a powerful machine learning method that combines the strengths of both gradient boosting and regularization techniques. By incorporating lasso and ridge shrinkage, it can mitigate overfitting and improve generalization performance. In this study, we utilized cross-validation to identify the optimal values for the L1 and L2 regularization parameters. We also used grid search to determine the optimal combination of hyperparameters, including the learning rate and the maximum tree depth. This approach allowed us to obtain the best possible predictive model for gold price fluctuations. The optimal XGBoost model achieved a test mean squared error (MSE) of 0.0000186 and a relative test MSE of 0.1928, indicating its high accuracy in predicting future gold price movements. These results demonstrate the effectiveness of the XGBoost algorithm in capturing complex relationships between variables and the target variable.

Overall, the XGBoost model provides a valuable tool for making informed decisions about gold investments. It's high accuracy and ability to handle complex relationships between variables make it a powerful tool for predicting future gold price fluctuations.

Figure 8: Scatterplot of Real vs. Predicted Gold Fluctuations

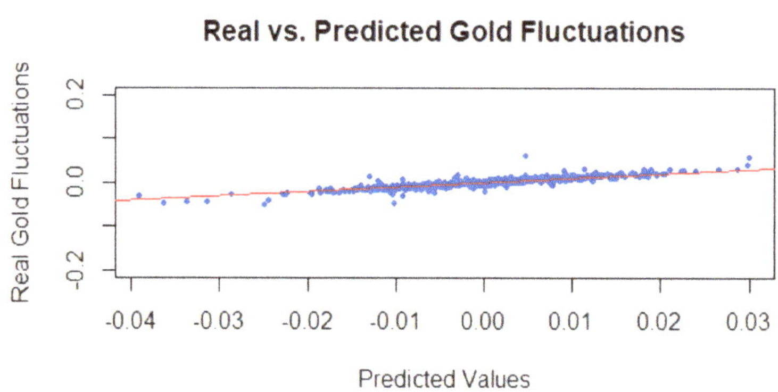

Figure 8 represents the relationship between the predicted values generated by our XGBoost model and the actual gold price movements. The scatter plot depicts the predicted values on the x-axis and the actual values on the y-axis. The 45-degree line, which represents a perfect match between the predicted and actual values, is also shown on the plot to highlight the strength of the relationship between the two. The plot shows that the predicted values are highly correlated with the actual values, with most of the points lying close to the 45-degree line. This indicates that the XGBoost model's predictions were accurate for a large number of data points. Moreover, the low variance of the distribution around the 45-degree line indicates that the model's predictions were consistently close to the actual values, making it a reliable tool for predicting future gold price movements.

5. Summary and Conclusions

In this study, we utilized various ML algorithms, including regression trees, random forests, GBRT, and XGBoost, to predict future gold price movements. The models were trained and tested on the same dataset, and their performance was evaluated using relative test mean squared error (RSE) and test mean squared error (MSE). We used a combination of major stock indices, leading 10 years bonds, and commodities such as oil and wheat as predictors in our models. Our results show that these ML algorithms can be effective tools for predicting gold price movements, with varying levels of accuracy. The examined models identified that gold three days Moving Average (MA) has the highest contribution to the current daily gold price movement followed by lagged data of gold from 1-4 prior days. The most influential stock indices are found to be one-day lagged data of ASX, S&P500, TA35, IBEX, and AEX. Out of the four countries 10 years' bond yields (US, Germany, France, and Japan), only U.S. and Japanese bond yields contributed information to gold price forecasting. Gas and silver have been found to have a delayed influence on current gold prices. Our models have also identified that one-day lagged VIX score and our VIX dummy variable have an important impact on gold price suggesting, that economic uncertainty influences gold price.

Our regression tree model achieved a relative test mean squared error (RSE) of 0.6401 and a test MSE of 0.000071772, indicating moderate accuracy in predicting future gold price movements. The random forest model achieved a relative test MSE of 0.43635 and a test MSE of 0.00004892, demonstrating a substantial improvement in accuracy compared to the regression tree. The GBRT model achieved a test MSE of 0.000018605 and a relative MSE of 0.16593, indicating a major improvement in accuracy compared to the random forest. Finally, the XGBoost model yielded a test MSE of 0.0000186 and a relative test MSE of 0.1928, also demonstrating a high level of accuracy in predicting gold price movements.

A comparative analysis of the above results indicates that all models achieved a considerable improvement in accuracy compared to the baseline regression tree model. The random forest model outperformed the regression tree model, achieving a substantial improvement in accuracy. The GBRT model achieved a major improvement in accuracy compared to the random forest, and the XGBoost model demonstrated the highest level of accuracy in predicting gold price movements. Despite the differences in the models' performance, there is a consensus that all models have the capability to accurately predict gold price fluctuations. The high accuracy of the models can be attributed to their ability to capture non-linear relationships between explanatory variables and the target variable and handle large datasets with multiple features.

Our study demonstrates the effectiveness of ML algorithms in predicting future gold price movements. Our models, particularly the GBRT and XGBoost models, achieved high levels of accuracy in predicting gold price movements, providing investors and financial analysts with a more accurate and reliable tool for making informed decisions about gold investments. The combination of raw data along with lagged MA and the VIX volatility index enabled to capture of complex relationships between the three examined financial markets: stocks, commodities, and bonds, providing important insight into the important role of gold as a hedging asset against economic risks.

The main limitations of our research are the lack of data from developing countries, the variety of bonds that were used, and the absence of cryptocurrencies, Future research should take into account a greater variety of bonds and stocks indices and major cryptocurrencies to further contribute to the knowledge of the role of gold in the global financial economy.

References

Adekoya, O.B., Oliyide, J.A., Olubiyi, E.A., Adedeji. A.O. (2023). The inflation-hedging performance of industrial metals in the world's most industrialized countries, Resources Policy, 81,103364.

Akhtaruzzaman, Md., Boubaker, S., Lucey, B M., Sensoy, A. (2021). Is gold a hedge or a safe-haven asset in the COVID–19 crisis? Economic Modelling, 102,105588.

Wen, F., Tong, X., Ren, X. (2022). Gold or Bitcoin, which is the safe haven during the COVID-19 pandemic? International Review of Financial Analysis, 81,102121.

Wang, K.M., Lee, Y.M. (2022). Is gold a safe haven for exchange rate risks? An empirical study of major currency countries, Journal of Multinational Financial Management, 63,100705.

Shahzad, S.J.H., Bouri, E., Rehman, M.U., Roubaud, D. (2022). The hedge asset for BRICS stock markets: Bitcoin, gold or VIX, The world economy, 45,1, 292-316.

Fakhfekh, M., Jerbi, A., Ghorbel, A., Hachicha, N. (2022). Hedging stock market prices with WTI, Gold, VIX and cryptocurrencies: a comparison between DCC, ADCC and GO-GARCH models. International journal of emerging markets. 18,4, 978-1006.

Elsayed, A.H., Gozgor, G., Yarovaya, L. (2022). Volatility and return connectedness of cryptocurrency, gold, and uncertainty: Evidence from the cryptocurrency uncertainty indices, Finance Research Letters, 47, B.

Zheng, Y. (2015). The linkage between aggregate investor sentiment and metal futures returns: A nonlinear approach. Q. Rev. Econ. Finance. 58, 128–142

Bosch, D., Pradkhan, E. (2015). The impact of speculation on precious metals futures markets. Resour. Policy. 44, 118–134.

Qadan, M. (2019). Risk appetite and the prices of precious metals. Resour. Policy, 62, 138–153.

Rehman, M.U., Hussain, S.J.H, Shahzad, Uddin, G.S., Hedström, A. (2018). Precious metal returns and oil shocks: A time varying connectedness approach, Resources Policy,58,77-89.

Wang, J., Li, X. (2018). A combined neural networks model for commodity price forecasting with SSA. Soft Computing, 22,5223-5233.

Kang, S.H.; McIver, R. (2017). Yoon, S.M. Dynamic spillover effects among crude oil, precious metal, and agricultural commodity futures markets. Energy Econ. 62, 19–32.

Akyildirim, E., Goncu, A., Sensoy, A. (2021). Prediction of cryptocurrency returns using machine learning. *Annals of Operational Res*earch. 297, 3–36.

Chen, K.; Zhou, Y.; Dai, F. A. (2015). LSTM-Based Method for Stock Returns Prediction: A Case Study of China Stock Market. In Proceedings of the IEEE International Conference on Big Data, Santa Clara, CA, USA, 2823–2824.

Borovkova, S.; Tsiamas, I. (20190. An ensemble of LSTM neural networks for high-frequency stock market classification. *J. Forecast. 38*, 600–619.

Fischer, T., Krauss, C. (2018). Deep learning with long short-term memory networks for financial market prediction. *European Journal of Operational Research*, 270, 2, 654-669.

Plakandaras, V., Ji, Q. (2022). Intrinsic decompositions in gold forecasting, Journal of Commodity Markets, 28,100245.

Zhang, P., Ci, B. (2020). Deep belief network for gold price forecasting, Resources Policy, 69,101806.

Vidal, A., Kristjanpoller, W. (2020). Gold volatility prediction using a CNN-LSTM approach, Expert Systems with Applications,157, 113481.

Alameer, Z., Elaziz, M.A., Ewees, A.A., Haiwang, Y., Zhang, J. (2019). Forecasting Copper Prices Using Hybrid Adaptive Neuro-Fuzzy. Inference System and Genetic Algorithms. Nat. Resour. Res 28, 1385-1401.

Livieris, I.E., Pintelas, E. & Pintelas, P. A. (2020). CNN–LSTM model for gold price time-series forecasting. Neural Comput & Applic 32, 17351–17360.

Jianwei, E., Jimin, Y., Haihong, J. (2019). A novel hybrid model on the prediction of time series and its application for the gold price analysis and forecasting, Physica A: Statistical Mechanics and its Applications, 527, 121454.

He, Z., Zhou, J., Dai, H.N., Wang, H. (2019). Gold Price Forecast Based on LSTM-CNN Model. IEEE Intl Conf on Dependable, Autonomic and Secure Computing, Intl Conf on Pervasive Intelligence and Computing, Intl Conf on Cloud and Big Data Computing, Intl Conf on Cyber Science and Technology Congress Fukuoka, Japan, 1046-1053.

Yu, B., Li, C., Mirza, N., Umar, M. (2022). Forecasting credit ratings of decarbonized firms: Comparative assessment of machine learning models, Technological Forecasting and Social Change, 174.

Ghosh, p., Neufeld, A., Sahoo, J.K. (2022). Forecasting directional movements of stock prices for intraday trading using LSTM and random forests, Finance Research Letters, 46, Part A,102280.

Derbentsex, D., Datsenko, N., babenko,V., Pushko,O., Pursky, O. (2020). Forecasting Cryptocurrencies Prices Using Ensembles-Based machine Learning Approach. IEEE International Conference on Problems of Info Communications. Science and Technology. Kharkiv, Ukraine, pp 707-712.

Appendix 1

A complete list of the selected explanatory variables from the stepwise selection includes the following: one, two, three, four, five, six, seven, eight and nine days lagged gold fluctuations, three, five and ten days moving averages of gold fluctuations, one, two and seven days lagged S&P fluctuations, one and two days lagged TA35 fluctuations, one and nine days lagged IBEX fluctuations, one, four, five, six, seven, eight and ten days lagged AEX fluctuations, one, four, five, six, seven, eight and ten days lagged fluctuations in BEL, one and eight days lagged ASX fluctuations, one day lagged VIX fluctuations, one, three and 10 days VIX dummy variable that receives the value of one if VIX is greater than 20, one and three days lagged fluctuations in US bonds yields, one day lagged fluctuations in Japan bonds yield, two and ten days lagged fluctuations in NSDQ, two, four, six, seven and eight days lagged Nifty fluctuations, two, three, four, five, six, seven, eight and nine lagged N225 fluctuations, three days lagged BVSP fluctuations, four and eight days lagged MOEX fluctuations, four and five days lagged SMI fluctuations, four and five days lagged HIS fluctuations, six and nine days lagged GAZ fluctuations, six, seven and nine days lagged FTSE fluctuations, seven days lagged SET fluctuations, eight, nine and ten days lagged Silver fluctuations, nine days lagged Wheat fluctuations, ten days lagged DAX and NZX fluctuations.

Predicting the Bitcoin's Price Using AI

Gil Cohen and Avishay Aiche*

Abstract

This study investigates the application of Artificial Intelligence (AI) and Machine Learning (ML) in predicting Bitcoin price movements and developing adaptive investment strategies. An analysis of Bitcoin performance from January 2018 to January 2024 revealed that the AI-driven strategy, leveraging an ensemble of neural networks, achieved a total return of 1640.32%, significantly surpassing the ML-based approach with a return of 304.77% and the traditional Buy-and-Hold (B&H) strategy at 223.40%. By incorporating predictive analytics and technical indicators, the AI strategy dynamically adjusted its market exposure, enabling it to mitigate losses during downturns and maximize gains during favorable market conditions. These findings underscore the transformative potential of AI in financial markets, particularly in emerging asset classes like cryptocurrencies. Using a broader spectrum of data and employing advanced analytical techniques, AI can provide a more nuanced understanding of market dynamics and investor behavior providing significant implications for portfolio management, risk assessment, and trading system design.

Keywords: Bitcoin, AI, Machine Learning, Random Forest.

*Gil Cohen and Avishay Aiche (avishaya@wgalil.ac.il) are from the Management Department, Western Galilee Academic College, Acre, Israel

Corresponding Author: Gil Cohen: gilc@wgalil.ac.il

1. Introduction

Artificial Intelligence (AI) has fundamentally reshaped the landscape of financial forecasting by offering unprecedented accuracy, efficiency, and adaptability. Unlike traditional statistical methods, which often rely on rigid assumptions and limited data, AI leverages machine learning algorithms capable of processing vast volumes of historical and real-time data. This enables AI to uncover complex, non-linear relationships and hidden patterns that human analysts or conventional models might overlook. As a result, AI-driven forecasting tools are increasingly used to predict market movements, assess risk, and develop sophisticated investment strategies (Feng, 2024). Moreover, AI systems are inherently dynamic, continuously learning from new data and adapting to changing market conditions, which enhances their predictive capabilities over time (Sari and Indrabudiman, 2024). One of the most significant advantages of AI in financial forecasting lies in its ability to integrate diverse data sources. In addition to traditional economic indicators such as interest rates, inflation, and GDP, AI can process unstructured data from news articles, social media platforms, and even geopolitical events. This holistic approach provides a more comprehensive view of market dynamics and investor sentiment, which is particularly valuable in volatile markets such as cryptocurrencies (Masood, 2024). In our research, we explored the potential of AI to predict Bitcoin's price trends and develop a profitable trading strategy. However, the use of AI in financial forecasting is not without challenges. One key concern is the reliability and quality of data, especially from unstructured sources like social media, which can be prone to misinformation and noise (Baviskar et al., 2021). Additionally, AI models are not immune to overfitting, where they may perform exceptionally well on historical data but fail to generalize to new market conditions. Therefore, continuous monitoring, validation, and refinement of AI models are crucial to ensure their long-term effectiveness.

Using ChatGPT to generate buy and sell signals optimizing entry and exit points in the BTC market through informed, data-driven decision-making, the AI was tasked with forecasting Bitcoin's price movements and optimizing a trading system based on these predictions. What sets this study apart is the AI's use of unconventional data sources, such as social media sentiment, in addition to traditional financial and economic data. This allowed the model to capture the real-time mood and behavior of market participants, which are critical drivers in the highly speculative cryptocurrency market. Results show that over the examined period from January 2018 to January 2024, the AI-driven strategy achieved a total return of 1640.32%, significantly surpassing the ML-based approach with a return of 304.77% and the traditional Buy-and-Hold (B&H) strategy at 223.40% (Masood, 2024). These findings underscore the transformative potential of AI in financial markets, particularly in emerging asset classes like cryptocurrencies. By leveraging a broader spectrum of data and employing advanced analytical techniques, AI can provide a more nuanced understanding of market dynamics and investor behavior and has significant implications for portfolio management, risk assessment, and trading system design.

2. Literature Review

The increasing complexity of financial markets, characterized by nonlinear dynamics, rapid fluctuations, and the interplay of numerous factors, has challenged the traditional statistical models once relied upon for forecasting (Jin et al., 2022; Navon and Keller, 2017). These conventional approaches often fail to capture the intricate temporal dependencies and evolving patterns that influence asset prices and market movements. In response, a growing body of literature demonstrates the superiority of Artificial Intelligence (AI) and Machine Learning (ML) techniques, particularly deep learning architectures, in predicting market trends with higher accuracy and robustness (Sonkavde, 2023; Wang et al., 2021; Razouk, 2023). Among deep learning frameworks, Recurrent Neural Networks (RNNs), Long Short-Term Memory (LSTM) networks, and Gated Recurrent Units (GRUs) have emerged as especially effective in modeling complex time-series data (Zhang, 2023; Deshpande, 2023). These models excel at learning and leveraging temporal dependencies, enabling them to detect subtle shifts in market behavior that might be missed by linear models or simpler algorithms. Research integrating these neural networks with complementary methods—such as empirical mode decomposition, convolutional neural networks, and reinforcement learning—has shown improved predictive capability and adaptability (Jin et al., 2022; Gao et al., 2020; Maeda et al., 2020). Beyond neural network approaches, scholars have explored various ML algorithms, including Support Vector Machines (SVMs), Artificial Neural Networks (ANNs), and ensemble methods like Random Forests (RF), Gradient Boosted Regression Trees (GBRT), and XGBoost, each of which can capture nonlinearities and complex variable interactions to improve forecasting accuracy (Pyo et al., 2017; Nabipour et al., 2020; Song et al., 2021).

The transition from traditional statistical forecasting to AI-driven methodologies capable of adapting to the evolving complexity of financial markets. By continually refining these approaches, including the integration of advanced ensemble methods, deep learning frameworks, and expanded data sources, researchers are pushing the boundaries of predictive accuracy. This ongoing progress contributes to the development of more informed and effective trading strategies, improving both risk management and decision-making (Wang et al., 2018; Gao et al., 2020; Wang, 2023). Integrating macroeconomic indicators, sentiment data derived from news or social media, and measures of market correlations and volatility such as the VIX provides a richer representation of the underlying forces shaping asset prices (Wang et al., 2021; Hu et al., 2021; Zaar et al., 2023). Studies also highlight the use of polynomial autoregression models, which can model nonlinear, speculative dynamics effectively (Bazán-Palomino and Svogun, 2023). As shown by Cohen (2024), polynomial moving regression bands can enhance automated trading systems, while Gradojevic and Kukolj (2023) identify RF as a particularly robust model for certain financial scenarios. Although these advancements significantly improve forecasting performance, the inherent noise and uncertainty in financial time series necessitate advanced preprocessing steps—such as denoising, feature engineering, and feature selection—to strengthen model reliability (Song et al., 2021; Hui et al., 2023).

Cryptocurrency markets present distinct challenges and opportunities for financial forecasting, often demanding specialized predictive approaches that can contend with heightened volatility, unique market drivers, and frequent structural changes. Unlike traditional equities, whose behavior is often influenced by relatively stable sets of macroeconomic variables and historical trends, cryptocurrencies are subject to a rapidly shifting landscape. Regulatory announcements, technological upgrades, social media sentiment, and changes in investor perception can trigger sudden price swings or emerging trading patterns. As a result, classical time-series models like ARIMA often falter when confronted with the nonlinear and stochastic nature of cryptocurrency price data (Derbentsev et al., 2019). ML and AI-driven models have shown considerable promise in cryptocurrency forecasting. Feature selection strategies enable the identification of the most relevant predictive indicators, while sentiment analysis and transaction pattern recognition provide nuanced insights into price formation and market behavior (Siva, 2024; Kwok, 2023). Deep learning architectures—such as RNNs, LSTMs, and GRUs—stand out as particularly well-suited for capturing the temporal complexity and nonlinearity of cryptocurrency time series (Saha, 2023; Hitam and Ismail, 2018). Giudici et al. (2024) extended the Shapley–Lorenz method, inherently normalized by design, to artificial intelligence models for time series of Bitcoin prices as the response variable, using traditional financial asset time series as explanatory variables. Their analysis reveals three main findings: first, recurrent neural networks outperform standard neural networks in terms of accuracy and robustness. Second, the most accurate models show that Bitcoin prices are primarily influenced by their own past values, with limited explanatory power from traditional financial assets. and third, despite this limited influence, recurrent neural networks effectively capture the contribution of classical assets to Bitcoin price prediction.

When combined with Natural Language Processing (NLP) techniques that extract signals from social media platforms and online forums, these models can dynamically integrate qualitative, unstructured data into quantitative forecasting frameworks (Girsang, 2023; Tollo et al., 2023). Ensemble methods, including stacking and boosting algorithms like XGBoost and LightGBM, further enhance predictive accuracy by aggregating the strengths of multiple base models. These ensemble-based approaches are particularly advantageous in the constantly evolving cryptocurrency environment, as they can readily incorporate a wide range of data sources ranging from blockchain network metrics to macroeconomic indicators while also capturing intricate variable interactions (Sun, 2024; Guan, 2022). This adaptability proves vital when grappling with limited historical data, sudden market irregularities, and the introduction of new digital assets with distinct behaviors. Babaei et al. (2022) proposed a methodology applied to a time series of portfolios constructed from a set of crypto assets, aiming to enhance the trustworthiness of robo-advisors. They assigned values to the predictions generated by a machine learning model, which was based on the outcomes of a dynamic Markowitz portfolio optimization model and offered explanations for the rationale behind the selected portfolio weights. Their findings suggest that this approach could serve as a valuable tool for regulators to assess the compliance of robo-advisory services with financial regulations.

The evaluation of portfolio performance is a critical aspect of investment management, with various metrics developed to assess risk-adjusted returns. The Sharpe ratio, quantifies the excess return per unit of risk, providing a straightforward method to compare the risk-adjusted performance of different portfolios (Leković, 2017; Nielsen and Vassalou, 2004). Jensen's alpha, on the other hand, measures the performance of a portfolio relative to its expected return based on the Capital Asset Pricing Model (CAPM). It represents the excess return that a portfolio generates over the expected return, given its systematic risk (beta) (Peck-Ling and Choong, 2022). Jensen's alpha is particularly useful for evaluating mutual fund managers' performance, as it isolates the impact of managerial skill from market movements (Nguyen et al., 2022). The significance of Jensen's alpha lies in its ability to provide a clearer picture of a manager's ability to generate returns above what is predicted by market risk. In this paper we used the Sharp ratio to compare the performances of the different strategies along with the length of time the strategies were exposed to the underlying asset (the Bitcoin).

3. Data and Methodologies

This study aims to develop a systematic trading algorithm for Bitcoin (BTC) using ChatGPT-o1 that integrates technical analysis, macroeconomic indicators, market sentiment, and machine learning techniques to generate buy and sell signals. The primary objective is to outperform the traditional buy-and-hold strategy by optimizing entry and exit points in the BTC market through informed, data-driven decision-making. Two distinct trading strategies were developed: one constructed solely by AI (ChatGPT-o1) and the other using traditional ML techniques without AI intervention. We compared the performance of these two strategies to better understand the contribution of AI in forecasting Bitcoin's price. Historical daily closing prices of BTC/USD were sourced from Yahoo Finance, covering the period from January 1, 2018, to January 1, 2024. This timeframe captures a variety of market conditions, including bullish runs and bearish downturns, providing a robust dataset for model development and evaluation. The Buy and Hold (B&H) strategy that is used as benchmark for performance evaluating is simply buying the Bitcoin at the beginning of the examined period (year or the entire period) and selling it at the end of the period.

This study aims to develop a systematic trading algorithm for Bitcoin (BTC) using ChatGPT-o1 that integrates technical analysis, macroeconomic indicators, market sentiment, and machine learning techniques to generate buy and sell signals. The primary objective is to outperform the traditional buy-and-hold strategy by optimizing entry and exit points in the BTC market through informed, data-driven decision-making. Two distinct trading strategies were developed: one constructed solely by AI (ChatGPT-o1) and the other using traditional ML techniques without AI intervention. We compared the performance of these two strategies to better understand the contribution of AI in forecasting Bitcoin's price.

Historical daily closing prices of BTC/USD were sourced from Yahoo Finance, covering the period from January 1, 2018, to January 1, 2024. This timeframe captures a variety of market conditions, including bullish runs and bearish downturns, providing a robust dataset for model development and evaluation. Table 1 presents summary statistics of Bitcoin’s daily and monthly returns, offering insight into the underlying volatility and market behavior over the examined period.

Table 1: Summary Statistics of Bitcoin's Daily and Monthly Returns (2018–2023)

Year	Mean Daily Return	SD Daily_Return	Mean Monthly Return	SD Monthly Return
2018	-0.264%	4.25%	-8.225%	22.52%
2019	0.242%	3.56%	6.862%	22.15%
2020	0.458%	3.77%	13.607%	24.77%
2021	0.216%	4.21%	4.772%	21.07%
2022	-0.226%	3.33%	-6.958%	15.56%
2023	0.283%	2.29%	8.146%	14.35%

The mean daily return fluctuates over the years, with negative values observed in 2018 (-0.264%) and 2022 (-0.226%), reflecting bearish market conditions, whereas positive returns dominate in 2019 (0.242%), 2020 (0.458%), 2021 (0.216%), and 2023 (0.283%). The standard deviation of daily returns ranges between 2.29% and 4.25%, indicating substantial volatility, particularly in 2018 and 2021. On a monthly level, mean returns exhibit more pronounced variability, with significant negative values in 2018 (-8.225%) and 2022 (-6.958%), and notably high positive returns in 2020 (13.607%) and 2023 (8.146%). The standard deviation of monthly returns further highlights the extreme price swings characteristic of Bitcoin, with the highest volatility recorded in 2020 (24.77%) and the lowest in 2023 (14.35%). These statistics confirm the necessity of employing adaptive and data-driven trading strategies, as Bitcoin's market behavior varies considerably across different years. The results also underscore the importance of incorporating risk-adjusted performance metrics in evaluating trading strategies, given the considerable fluctuations in return distributions over time.

The Buy and Hold (B&H) strategy, which serves as a benchmark for performance evaluation, consists of purchasing Bitcoin at the beginning of the examined period (either annually or for the entire period) and selling it at the end. This simple yet widely used strategy provides a baseline for assessing the effectiveness of AI-driven and ML-based trading approaches in different market conditions.

3.1 Indicators and Trading Strategy of ChatGPT-o1

To capture market momentum and potential trend reversals, two widely recognized technical indicators were utilized: the Relative Strength Index (RSI) and the Moving Average Convergence Divergence (MACD). The RSI was calculated using a 14-day period, a standard choice that balances sensitivity with noise reduction. Market sentiment was measured using Google Trends data for the keyword "Bitcoin," accessed via the Pytrends API. A 7-day rolling means of search interest was calculated to smooth out daily fluctuations while maintaining sensitivity to shifts in public interest. When the current search interest exceeded the 7-day mean, it was interpreted as increasing market interest, generating a bullish signal (+1). Conversely, if the search interest fell below or equaled the 7-day mean, it indicated declining interest and produced a bearish signal (-1). This method captures the collective sentiment of market participants, which can significantly influence Bitcoin's price, given its speculative nature. A Random Forest Classifier was employed to incorporate predictive analytics into the trading strategy. This algorithm was chosen for its robustness, ability to handle nonlinear relationships, and effectiveness in classification tasks. The features used for the machine learning model included technical indicators (RSI and MACD), macroeconomic variables, and Google Trends search interest. The target variable was a binary indicator of the next day's price movement, set to 1 if the price was expected to increase and 0 if not. To avoid look-ahead bias and ensure that the model's predictions were based only on information available at the time, a rolling window approach was applied for model training.

The trading strategy was initialized with a starting capital of $10,000, held entirely in cash at the outset. The algorithm's trading decisions were based on the weighted score, with specific rules for buying, selling, and holding positions. When the weighted score exceeded 0.5 and the algorithm was not currently holding BTC, it would invest the entire available capital in Bitcoin at the closing price, effectively executing a buy order. If the weighted score fell below -0.5 and the algorithm was holding BTC, it would liquidate the entire position at the closing price, executing a sell order. If the weighted score was between -0.5 and 0.5, the algorithm would hold the current position, whether in cash or BTC. Return values were calculated based on the holdings and current BTC price. If the algorithm was holding BTC, the strategy value was the product of the BTC units held and the current price. If not holding BTC, the strategy value equaled the available cash. For simplification, transaction costs, slippage, and taxes were not considered in the calculations.

3.2 Neural Networks Approach

In comparison with the AI method, this study constructs a systematic trading strategy for Bitcoin by integrating advanced neural network architectures with technical analysis. The dataset consists of daily Bitcoin price and volume information obtained from Yahoo Finance, covering the period from January 2018 to January 2024. This timeframe captures various market conditions, including high volatility, sustained bullish trends, and periods of decline, ensuring a robust evaluation of the models.

To preprocess the data, missing values were forward-filled to maintain continuity, and date indices and time zones were standardized for consistency. Outliers were not explicitly removed but were smoothed through the application of Simple Moving Averages (SMA) and Bollinger Bands, reducing noise in the data.

The training, validation, and testing framework was designed to ensure real-time predictive performance without introducing look-ahead bias. A rolling window methodology was implemented, where the model was trained on the preceding ten days of Bitcoin price data. During hyperparameter tuning, five-fold cross-validation was performed within the training window to prevent overfitting. Once trained, the model generated a prediction for the following day's price movement using only historical data available at the time. After each day, the window moved forward by one observation, discarding the earliest data point and incorporating the most recent one. This rolling approach ensured that the model continuously adapted to new market conditions, improving its ability to generalize across different trading environments.

To capture the complexities of financial time-series data, three distinct neural network architectures were employed: a feedforward neural network (FNN), a Long Short-Term Memory (LSTM) network, and a Gated Recurrent Unit (GRU) network. The feedforward neural network served as the baseline model, consisting of three hidden layers, with the number of neurons per layer ranging between 32 and 128. The activation function used within the hidden layers was ReLU, chosen for its non-linearity and computational efficiency, while the output layer employed a sigmoid activation function to generate probabilistic price movement predictions. The LSTM network was incorporated due to its capacity to retain and utilize information over long sequences, making it particularly well-suited for financial time-series analysis. This model consisted of two layers with 50 neurons per layer, and dropout regularization was applied at a rate of 0.2 to mitigate overfitting. The Adam optimizer was used to ensure rapid convergence of the model's parameters. The GRU network, a variant of LSTM with a simplified gating mechanism, consisted of two layers with 40 neurons per layer. Batch normalization was applied to stabilize and accelerate training while ensuring robust performance across varying market conditions.

To enhance predictive accuracy, the outputs of the three models were aggregated using a weighted ensemble approach, with the feedforward neural network assigned a weight of 0.4, while the LSTM and GRU networks were each given a weight of 0.3. Hyperparameter optimization was conducted using a systematic grid search approach, refining parameters such as the learning rate (ranging from 0.001 to 0.01), batch size (ranging from 16 to 64), and number of epochs (up to 200) to balance predictive accuracy and generalization.

Trading decisions were based on the aggregated probability predictions of the ensemble model. A buy signal was issued when the probability of a price increase exceeded 0.6, whereas a sell signal was triggered when the probability fell below 0.4. If the probability remained between 0.4 and 0.6, a hold decision was made. To further refine the decision-making process, traditional technical indicators were integrated into the strategy. SMA crossovers were used to confirm trends, ensuring that buy signals were executed only when the short-term SMA exceeded the long-term SMA. Bollinger Bands provided additional validation by preventing buy signals when the price was above the upper Bollinger Band and suppressing sell signals when it was below the lower Bollinger Band.

Despite the complexity of these models, computational efficiency remained a key strength of the methodology. Each iteration, including training and prediction, was completed within seconds, making the strategy feasible for real-time trading applications. The model’s performance was evaluated using several key metrics, including the F1 score, which achieved a value of 0.85, demonstrating strong predictive reliability. Additionally, Sharpe ratio and maximum drawdown were used to assess the profitability and risk-adjusted performance of the strategy. This comprehensive evaluation framework ensures that the methodology remains both theoretically sound and practically viable in live trading scenarios.

4. Results

The development of this trading algorithm, generated by the AI (ChatGPT o1), highlights the potential benefits of combining technical analysis, market sentiment, and machine learning in financial decision-making. The careful selection and optimization of parameters, especially the weights assigned to each signal, were key to improving the algorithm's performance. By integrating traditional indicators with advanced predictive techniques, the algorithm effectively identified profitable trading opportunities and managed risk, consistently outperforming the buy-and-hold strategy over the analysis period.

4.1 Signal Integration and Weighted Score Calculation

The trading algorithm integrated the signals from the RSI, MACD, Google Trends, and the machine learning model into a single weighted score. This score was used to generate buy or sell signals based on predefined thresholds. The weights assigned to each component were crucial in determining the influence of each signal on the final decision. Initially, the weights were set as follows: RSI Signal at 30%, MACD Signal at 30%, Google Trends Signal at 20%, and ML Signal at 20%. These weights were chosen based on domain expertise and the relative importance of each signal. The higher weights assigned to the RSI and MACD signals reflect their established effectiveness in technical analysis, emphasizing the algorithm's responsiveness to price momentum and trend reversals. The Google Trends and ML signals were given slightly lower weights to balance traditional analysis with market sentiment and predictive insights.

The weighted score at time *t* was calculated using the formula:

$$\begin{aligned} &Weighted\ Score_t \\ &= 0.2 * RSI\ Signal_t + 0.4 * MACD\ Signal_t + 0.2 \\ &* Google\ Trends\ Signal_t + 0.4 * ML\ Signal_t \end{aligned} \tag{1}$$

A weighted score greater than 0.5 signaled a strong buy recommendation, while a score less than -0.5 indicated a strong sell recommendation. Scores between -0.5 and 0.5 suggested holding the current position. The thresholds were set to ensure that only strong, corroborated signals prompted trading actions, reducing the likelihood of false positives due to market noise. Table 1 presents the results of the AI strategy performances compared to the B&H strategy.

4.2 A Comparison Between Performance of the AI VS Buy and Hold Strategies

Table 2: Performances of AI and B&H Strategies (2018-2023)

Date	AI Return	B&H Return	AI Annual Return	B&H Annual Return	Excess Return AI
2018-02	0.00%	1.73%			
2018-03	0.00%	-32.93%			
2018-04	11.41%	32.51%			
2018-05	-9.43%	-18.90%			
2018-06	0.00%	-14.55%			
2018-07	4.20%	21.49%			
2018-08	-15.58%	-9.55%			
2018-09	0.00%	-5.85%			
2018-10	0.00%	-4.65%			
2018-11	0.00%	-36.41%			
2018-12	0.00%	-6.83%	**-11.24%**	**-71.85%**	**60.61%**
2019-01	0.00%	-7.61%			
2019-02	-2.51%	11.48%			
2019-03	6.50%	6.50%			
2019-04	30.33%	30.33%			
2019-05	60.25%	60.25%			
2019-06	26.15%	26.15%			
2019-07	-8.37%	-6.76%			
2019-08	-18.42%	-4.51%			
2019-09	10.01%	-13.88%			
2019-10	0.00%	10.92%			
2019-11	-17.53%	-17.72%			
2019-12	0.00%	-4.97%	**85.52%**	**87.33%**	**-1.81%**
2020-01	7.40%	29.98%			
2020-02	-6.05%	-8.03%			
2020-03	0.00%	-25.13%			
2020-04	21.66%	34.48%			
2020-05	9.27%	9.27%			
2020-06	-2.86%	-3.41%			
2020-07	18.19%	23.92%			

2020-08	3.16%	3.16%			
2020-09	-12.29%	-7.67%			
2020-10	19.88%	27.79%			
2020-11	42.41%	42.41%			
2020-12	47.77%	47.77%	**251.54%**	**307.96%**	**-56.42%**
2021-01	14.18%	14.18%			
2021-02	36.31%	36.31%			
2021-03	30.53%	30.53%			
2021-04	-12.15%	-1.98%			
2021-05	0.00%	-35.35%			
2021-06	0.00%	-6.14%			
2021-07	4.04%	18.79%			
2021-08	13.31%	13.31%			
2021-09	-7.16%	-7.16%			
2021-10	40.03%	40.03%			
2021-11	-6.12%	-7.03%			
2021-12	0.00%	-18.77%	**156.82%**	**62.34%**	**94.48%**
2022-01	0.00%	-16.89%			
2022-02	-0.85%	12.24%			
2022-03	-5.51%	5.43%			
2022-04	-10.95%	-17.18%			
2022-05	0.00%	-15.70%			
2022-06	0.00%	-37.77%			
2022-07	0.00%	17.95%			
2022-08	-5.99%	-14.09%			
2022-09	0.00%	-3.08%			
2022-10	0.00%	5.48%			
2022-11	-14.64%	-16.23%			
2022-12	-2.98%	-3.62%	**-35.05%**	**-65.13%**	**30.08%**
2023-01	22.63%	39.84%			
2023-02	0.03%	0.03%			
2023-03	2.78%	23.03%			
2023-04	2.78%	2.78%			
2023-05	-7.75%	-7.00%			
2023-06	0.10%	11.97%			
2023-07	-4.09%	-4.09%			
2023-08	0.00%	-11.29%			
2023-09	0.21%	4.00%			
2023-10	28.55%	28.55%			
2023-11	8.78%	8.78%			
2023-12	12.07%	12.07%	**80.24%**	**155.42%**	**-75.18%**
Overall Return	**1640.32%**	**223.40%**			**1416.92%**

Notes: AI and B&H returns are monthly returns calculated at the end of each month.

Table 2 illustrates that the AI-driven strategy significantly outperformed the Buy-and-Hold (B&H) strategy, yielding a total return of 1640.32% over the analyzed period, compared to a return of 223.40% achieved by the B&H strategy. Over the examined period, the price of Bitcoin increased from $13,657.20 on January 1, 2018, to $44,167.33 on January 1, 2024. After accounting for trading costs of 1% per transaction and considering the 51 trades executed by the AI strategy, the net profit is adjusted to 1589.32%. The only years in which the Buy-and-Hold (B&H) strategy outperformed the AI-driven strategy were 2020 and 2023, while in 2019, both strategies delivered similar returns. Our AI strategy outperformed the Buy and Hold (B&H) strategy during periods of relatively high volatility for Bitcoin, particularly in 2018 and 2021-2022. However, the B&H strategy outperformed the AI strategy in years of less volatile price increases, specifically in 2020 and 2023. In 2020, Bitcoin experienced a unique convergence of events that significantly influenced its global adoption and perception. In 2023, Bitcoin began a strong recovery from the previous year, driven by several key factors. Institutional interest surged as major financial institutions like BlackRock and Fidelity filed applications for Bitcoin exchange-traded funds (ETFs), signaling a potential gateway for mainstream investment once approved.

To provide a visual representation of the AI strategy's performance, Figure 1 illustrates the strategy's performance over time, starting with an initial investment of $10,000. The graph highlights the substantial growth achieved by the AI-driven strategy, showcasing its ability to navigate varying market conditions and deliver significant returns.

4.2 A Comparison Between Performance of the ML VS Buy and Hold Strategies

Table 3: Performances of ML and B&H Strategies (2018-2023)

Date	ML Return	B&H Return	ML Annual Return	B&H Annual Return	Excess Return ML
2018-02	0.00%	1.73%			
2018-03	-22.44%	-32.93%			
2018-04	0.00%	32.51%			
2018-05	-26.09%	-18.90%			
2018-06	0.00%	-14.55%			
2018-07	-5.03%	21.49%			

2018-08	-13.70%	-9.55%			
2018-09	0.00%	-5.85%			
2018-10	0.00%	-4.65%			
2018-11	0.00%	-36.41%			
2018-12	0.00%	-6.83%	**-53.95%**	**-71.85%**	**17.90%**
2019-01	-10.50%	-7.61%			
2019-02	-3.76%	11.48%			
2019-03	6.37%	6.50%			
2019-04	28.68%	30.33%			
2019-05	58.71%	60.25%			
2019-06	26.31%	26.15%			
2019-07	-10.05%	-6.76%			
2019-08	0.00%	-4.51%			
2019-09	0.00%	-13.88%			
2019-10	0.00%	10.92%			
2019-11	-22.74%	-17.72%			
2019-12	0.00%	-4.97%	**64.33%**	**87.33%**	**-23.00%**
2020-01	7.18%	29.98%			
2020-02	-8.45%	-8.03%			
2020-03	4.06%	-25.13%			
2020-04	25.82%	34.48%			
2020-05	6.73%	9.27%			
2020-06	-9.60%	-3.41%			
2020-07	0.00%	23.92%			
2020-08	-0.67%	3.16%			
2020-09	-13.43%	-7.67%			
2020-10	20.57%	27.79%			
2020-11	42.87%	42.41%			
2020-12	54.24%	47.77%	**216.75%**	**307.96%**	**-91.21%**
2021-01	12.73%	14.18%			
2021-02	34.59%	36.31%			
2021-03	18.71%	30.53%			
2021-04	-7.23%	-1.98%			
2021-05	0.00%	-35.35%			
2021-06	0.00%	-6.14%			
2021-07	0.00%	18.79%			
2021-08	5.86%	13.31%			
2021-09	-8.09%	-7.16%			
2021-10	6.67%	40.03%			
2021-11	-6.16%	-7.03%			
2021-12	0.00%	-18.77%	**87.29%**	**62.34%**	**24.95%**
2022-01	0.00%	-16.89%			
2022-02	12.39%	12.24%			

2022-03	-16.97%	5.43%			
2022-04	-14.13%	-17.18%			
2022-05	0.00%	-15.70%			
2022-06	0.00%	-37.77%			
2022-07	-2.13%	17.95%			
2022-08	-12.94%	-14.09%			
2022-09	0.00%	-3.08%			
2022-10	0.00%	5.48%			
2022-11	-17.31%	-16.23%			
2022-12	-1.75%	-3.62%	**-42.16%**	**-65.13%**	**22.97%**
2023-01	9.71%	39.84%			
2023-02	-2.43%	0.03%			
2023-03	4.19%	23.03%			
2023-04	3.02%	2.78%			
2023-05	-1.54%	-7.00%			
2023-06	-0.01%	11.97%			
2023-07	-4.45%	-4.09%			
2023-08	-1.67%	-11.29%			
2023-09	0.00%	4.00%			
2023-10	26.39%	28.55%			
2023-11	6.42%	8.78%			
2023-12	12.07%	12.07%	**67.35%**	**155.42%**	**-88.07%**
Overall Return	**304.77%**	**223.40%**			**81.37%**

Notes: ML returns and B&H returns are monthly returns calculated at the end of each month.

Table 3 shows that the machine learning (ML) strategy achieved a total return of 304.77%, significantly outperforming the Buy-and-Hold (B&H) strategy, which yielded a return of 223.40%. Accounting for the 22 trades executed by the ML algorithm, with a transaction cost of 1% per trade, the net return of the ML strategy was adjusted to 282.77%. This substantial outperformance highlights the efficacy of the ML-driven approach in predicting the highly volatile cryptocurrency market. The superior results of the ML strategy can be attributed to its dynamic asset allocation strategy, which adeptly reduces exposure during market downturns. Unlike the B&H strategy, which maintains a static position irrespective of market conditions, the ML strategy dynamically adjusts its exposure based on predictive analytics derived from a scoring mechanism generated by three neural networks. This adaptability allows the ML strategy to minimize losses during bearish market phases, thereby preserving capital and enhancing overall returns.

To illustrate the performance of the ML strategy, Figure 1 presents its value over time, starting with an initial investment of $10,000. The graph highlights the strategies' growth trajectory from 2018 to 2023, showcasing its ability to adapt dynamically to varying market conditions and maintain resilience during periods of heightened volatility.

Figure 1: AI vs. ML Strategy Performance starting with an initial investment of $10,000, over the period 2018–2023

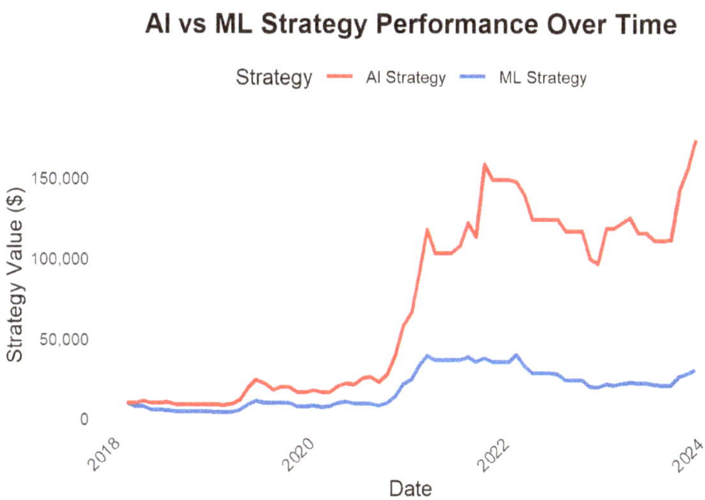

Table 4 presents a detailed comparison of the annual returns achieved by the AI-driven strategy, the ML-driven strategy, and the Buy-and-Hold (B&H) strategy across the years 2018 to 2023. The results highlight the relative performance advantages of the AI and ML strategies over the static B&H approach. Notably, the AI strategy outperformed the B&H strategy in all years except 2020 and 2023, showcasing its ability to dynamically adjust to market conditions. For instance, in 2018, a particularly challenging year for cryptocurrency markets, the AI strategy managed a smaller loss of -11.24% compared to the B&H strategy's -71.85%, yielding an AI return over B&H of 60.61%. Similarly, the ML strategy also demonstrated resilience in 2018 with a loss of -53.95%, outperforming the B&H strategy but underperforming the AI strategy by 42.71%. In years with strong bullish trends, such as 2021, the AI strategy recorded a return of 156.82%, surpassing both the ML strategy at 87.29% and the B&H strategy at 62.34%. This reflects the AI strategy's capacity to capitalize on upward market momentum more effectively than its counterparts. However, in years such as 2020 and 2023, the B&H strategy outperformed both the AI and ML strategies, with returns of

307.96% and 155.42%, respectively. These results suggest that in extreme bullish conditions, the static exposure of the B&H strategy can sometimes yield higher returns due to its full market participation. Comparative metrics also reveal the relationship between the AI and ML strategies. The AI strategy consistently outperformed the ML strategy across all years except 2019, where their performances were closely aligned, with the ML strategy returning 64.33% compared to the AI strategy's 85.52%. This consistent advantage is attributable to the AI strategy's superior adaptability and more refined predictive analytics, which enable it to navigate both bullish and bearish phases more effectively. Overall, Table 4 highlights the advantages of dynamic, machine-learning-based strategies in navigating the complexities of cryptocurrency markets.

Table 4: Performances of AI, ML, B&H Strategies (2018-2023)

Date	AI	ML	B&H	AI Return Over B&H	ML Return Over B&H	AI Return Over ML
2018	-11.24%	-53.95%	-71.85%	60.61%	17.90%	42.71%
2019	85.52%	64.33%	87.33%	-1.81%	-23.00%	21.19%
2020	251.54%	216.75%	307.96%	-56.42%	-91.21%	34.79%
2021	156.82%	87.29%	62.34%	94.48%	24.95%	69.53%
2022	-35.05%	-42.16%	-65.13%	30.08%	22.97%	7.11%
2023	80.24%	67.35%	155.42%	-75.18%	-88.07%	12.89%

Notes: The results presented in the table are annual returns.

The comparative analysis of annual returns provides a solid foundation for evaluating the risk profiles of these strategies. This is further illustrated by the number of days Bitcoin was held in each strategy, offering additional insights into their exposure to market volatility and risk management approaches. The comparison of Bitcoin holding number of days across the strategies highlights their differing levels of market exposure and associated risk. The Machine Learning (ML) strategy, developed in this study, held Bitcoin for 1,057 days, while the GPT-o1 strategy held it for 2,083 days. By contrast, the Buy-and-Hold (B&H) strategy maintained a position throughout the entire evaluation period of 2,192 days. Holding days serve as a measure of exposure to market volatility; fewer days indicate a more conservative approach with reduced risk. The ML strategy's lower holding days demonstrate its ability to limit exposure while achieving substantial returns. On the other hand, the GPT-o1 strategy, which achieved the highest profits, displayed a more aggressive stance with greater exposure. The B&H strategy, with continuous exposure, represents the riskiest approach. These results underscore the importance of adaptive strategies in managing risk while optimizing returns in highly volatile markets like cryptocurrencies.

Table 5: Annualized Monthly Returns and Sharpe Ratios for AI, ML, and B&H Strategies (2018–2023)

Year	AI	ML	B&H	AI -Sharp Ratio	ML -Sharp Ratio	B&H -Sharp Ratio
2018	-0.86%	-6.11%	-8.22%	-3.80%	-27.15%	-36.52%
2019	7.20%	6.08%	6.86%	32.50%	27.46%	30.97%
2020	12.38%	10.78%	13.61%	49.97%	43.51%	54.93%
2021	9.42%	4.76%	4.77%	44.69%	22.58%	22.65%
2022	-3.41%	-4.40%	-6.96%	-21.91%	-28.30%	-44.72%
2023	5.51%	4.31%	8.15%	38.39%	30.03%	56.78%

Table 5 presents the annualized average monthly returns and Sharpe ratios for the AI, ML, and Buy-and-Hold (B&H) strategies from 2018 to 2023. The results highlight the relative performance and risk-adjusted efficiency of each trading approach in different market conditions.

The AI strategy consistently delivers higher average returns than ML across most years, particularly in 2021 (9.42% vs. 4.76%) and 2023 (5.51% vs. 4.31%), demonstrating its superior ability to capture profitable trading opportunities. However, the B&H strategy outperforms both AI and ML in 2020 (13.61%) and 2023 (8.15%), reflecting the strong bullish trends during those years, where passive holding benefited from prolonged price surges.

The Sharpe ratios reveal critical insights into the risk-adjusted performance of each strategy. The AI strategy consistently achieves higher Sharpe ratios than ML, confirming that it generates superior returns relative to its volatility. Notably, in 2021, the AI strategy records a Sharpe ratio of 44.69%, nearly twice that of ML (22.58%) and significantly higher than B&H (22.65%), showcasing its ability to maximize returns while maintaining a favorable risk profile.

In bearish years such as 2018 and 2022, all strategies suffer negative returns, with B&H performing the worst in 2022 (-6.96%). However, AI maintains a less negative Sharpe ratio (-21.91%) compared to ML (-28.30%) and B&H (-44.72%), suggesting a more effective risk management mechanism during downturns.

These findings underscore the robustness of AI-driven strategies in adapting to various market conditions. While B&H capitalizes on long-term bullish trends, it exposes investors to higher volatility and drawdowns during market declines. The AI strategy, in contrast, exhibits a more balanced risk-return tradeoff, particularly in high-volatility environments, making it a compelling alternative for Bitcoin trading.

5. Contributions and Limitations of ChatGPT in Financial Analysis

AI-driven investment forecasting offers powerful benefits, such as the ability to analyze vast, diverse datasets in real time, detect subtle patterns beyond human capability, reduce emotional bias, and automate routine tasks ultimately improving decision-making speed and scalability. ChatGPT-o1 contributed significantly to the design of the trading strategy by recommending the use of technical indicators, sentiment analysis, and machine learning algorithms tailored for Bitcoin price prediction. Techniques such as the RSI, MACD, and Google Trends data were selected for their proven effectiveness in capturing short and medium term market trends. The use of a Random Forest Classifier was particularly valuable for integrating diverse features, including technical indicators, macroeconomic variables, and sentiment data. The rolling window approach ensured that predictions were based exclusively on available information, mitigating risks associated with look ahead bias. However, ChatGPT's capabilities are limited by its focus on linguistic models, as it cannot independently solve mathematical problems or account for individual investment preferences, such as risk tolerance or liquidity constraints. Its recommendations, while technically robust, may not align with the specific goals or financial contexts of individual investors. Moreover, the dependence on data quality, the risk of overfitting or replicating historical biases, regulatory complications, and the potential for systemic risk if many market participants rely on similar AI strategies. Striking a balance between human oversight and automated analytics, alongside strong validation and regulatory compliance, is vital for harnessing the advantages while mitigating the inherent risks.

6. Summary and Conclusions

In this paper, we examine the effectiveness of Artificial Intelligence (AI) and Machine Learning (ML) strategies in predicting Bitcoin price movements. The first strategy, employing an AI-driven approach with an ensemble of neural networks, achieved an exceptional total return of 1640.32% over the examined period from January 2018 to January 2024. The second strategy, using a machine learning-based algorithm (ML) driven by neural network ensembles and trading daily, produced a total return of 304.77% over the same period. Both strategies significantly outperformed the traditional Buy-and-Hold (B&H) strategy, which yielded a return of 223.40%. When accounting for trading costs of 0.5% per transaction, the AI strategy maintained an impressive return of 1589.32%, while the ML strategy achieved an adjusted return of 282.77%. The superior performance of the AI-driven strategy can be attributed to its dynamic and adaptive trading mechanism, which leverages predictive analytics from three neural network architectures: feedforward neural networks, LSTM, and GRU. This ensemble allowed the AI strategy to capture complex market patterns and dynamically adjust exposure during volatile market phases, thereby preserving capital during downturns and enhancing gains during bullish trends. Meanwhile, the ML strategy demonstrated robust performance, consistently outperforming the B&H strategy in most years, despite being slightly less effective than the AI strategy in optimizing risk-adjusted returns. A key advantage of both AI and ML strategies is their ability to mitigate losses during bearish market conditions. For instance, in 2022, a particularly challenging year, the AI strategy limited losses to -35.05% compared to -65.13% for the B&H strategy, showcasing the model's effectiveness in preserving capital. Similarly, the ML strategy limited losses to -42.16%, highlighting its adaptive risk management capabilities. The AI strategy's dynamic asset allocation, supported by technical indicators and ensemble modeling, proved particularly effective in navigating the volatile cryptocurrency market. This study underscores the potential of AI-driven strategies to achieve superior returns through enhanced predictive accuracy and adaptive decision-making. The findings suggest that integrating machine learning models with traditional financial analysis can provide investors with a powerful toolkit for navigating complex and volatile markets.

The authors state equal contribution for this paper.

References

Babaei, G., Giudici, P., Raffinetti, E. (2022). Explainable Artificial Intelligence for crypto asset allocation. Finance Research Letters, 47, 102941.

Bazán-Palomino, W., Svogun, D. (2023). On the drivers of technical analysis profits in cryptocurrency markets: A Distributed Lag approach, International Review of Financial Analysis, 86, 102516.

Cohen,G. (2024). Polynomial Moving Regression Band Stocks Trading System. Risks, 12,10,15-1.

Derbentsev, V., Datsenko, N., Степаненко, O., Bezkorovainyi, V. (2019). Forecasting cryptocurrency prices time series using machine learning approach. SHS Web of Conferences, 65, 02001. https://doi.org/10.1051/shsconf/20196502001

Deshpande, V. (2023). Implementation of long short-term memory (LSTM) networks for stock price prediction. RJCSE, 4(2), 60-72.

Gao, Z., Gao, Y., Hu, Y., Jiang, Z., Su, J. (2020). Application of deep q-network in portfolio management., 268-275.

Girsang, A. (2023). Hybrid LSTM and GRU for cryptocurrency price forecasting based on social network sentiment analysis using Finbert. Ieee Access, 11, 120530-120540.

Giudici, P., Piergallini, A., Recchioni, M.C., Raffinetti, E. (2024). Explainable AI methods for financial time series. Physica A: Statistical Mechanics with applications, 655, 130176

Gradojevic, N., Kukolj, D., Adcock, R. (2023). Vladimir Djakovic, Forecasting Bitcoin with technical analysis: A not-so-random forest? International Journal of Forecasting, 39, 1, 1-17.

Guan, Y. (2022). The price prediction for cryptocurrency based on the state-of-art machine learning approaches. BCP Business שמג Management, 23, 567-572.

Hitam, N., Ismail, A. (2018). Comparative performance of machine learning algorithms for cryptocurrency forecasting. Indonesian Journal of Electrical Engineering and Computer Science, 11(3), 1121.

Hu, Z., Zhao, Y., & Khushi, M. (2021). A survey of forex and stock price prediction using deep learning. Applied System Innovation, 4(1), 9.

Hui, X., Sun, B., Zhou, Y., & Sengupta, I. (2023). Stochastic volatility modeling of high-frequency CSI 300 index and dynamic jump prediction driven by machine learning. Electric Research Archive. https://doi.org/10.48550/arxiv.2204.02891

Jin, Z., Jin, Y., Chen, Z. (2022). Empirical mode decomposition using deep learning model for financial market forecasting. Peerj Computer Science, 8, e1076.

Kwok, T. (2023). An empirical analysis of forecasting bitcoin and gold price using arima model. Advances in Economics Management and Political Sciences, 46(1), 164-174.

Leković, M. (2017). Mutual funds portfolio performance evaluation models: sharpe, treynor and jensen index. Bankarstvo, 46(4), 108-133.

Maeda, I., deGraw, D., Kitano, M., Matsushima, H., Sakaji, H., Izumi, K., … Kato, A. (2020). Deep reinforcement learning in agent based financial market simulation. Journal of Risk and Financial Management, 13(4), 71.

Nabipour, M., Nayyeri, P., Jabani, H., Shahab, S., Mosavi, A. (2020). Predicting stock market trends using machine learning and deep learning algorithms via continuous and binary data; a comparative analysis. Ieee Access, 8, 150199-150212.

Navon, A., Keller,Y. (2017). Financial time series prediction using deep learning. Electric Research Archive. https://doi.org/10.48550/arxiv.1711.04174.

Nguyen, N., Trung, N., Thalassinos, E., and Le, H. (2022). The performance of shrinkage estimator for stock portfolio selection in case of high dimensionality. Journal of Risk and Financial Management, 15(6), 249.

Nielsen, L. and Vassalou, M. (2004). Sharpe ratios and alphas in continuous time. Journal of Financial and Quantitative Analysis, 39(1), 103-114.

Patel, J., Kalariya, V., Parmar, P., Tanwar, S., Kumar, N., Alazab, M. (2020). Stochastic neural networks for cryptocurrency price prediction. Ieee Access, 8, 82804-82818.

Peck-Ling, T. and Choong, S. (2022). Determinants of malaysian real estate investment trusts (m-reits) risk-adjusted performance during the period of property oversupply. Journal of Contemporary Issues and Thought, 12(1), 10-23.

Pyo, S., Lee, J., Cha, M., & Jang, H. (2017). Predictability of machine learning techniques to forecast the trends of market index prices: hypothesis testing for the korean stock markets. Plos One, 12(11), e0188107.

Razouk, A. (2023). Performance evaluation of technical indicators for forecasting the Moroccan stock index using deep learning. Indonesian Journal of Electrical Engineering and Computer Science, 32(3), 1785.

Saha, V. (2023). Predicting future cryptocurrency prices using machine learning algorithms. Journal of Data Analysis and Information Processing, 11(04), 400-419.

Siva, R. (2024). Analyzing the machine learning methods to predict bitcoin pricing. World Journal of Advanced Research and Reviews, 21(1), 1288-1294.

Song, D., Baek, A., Kim, N. (2021). Forecasting stock market indices using padding-based fourier transform denoising and time series deep learning models. Ieee Access, 9, 83786-83796.

Sonkavde, G. (2023). Forecasting stock market prices using machine learning and deep learning models: a systematic review, performance analysis and discussion of implications. International Journal of Financial Studies, 11(3), 94.

Sun, G. (2024). Cryptocurrency price prediction based on Xboost, Lightgbm and BNN. Applied and Computational Engineering, 49(1), 273-279.

Tollo, G., Andria, J., Filograsso, G. (2023). The predictive power of social media sentiment: evidence from cryptocurrencies and stock markets using NLP and stochastic Anns. Mathematics, 11(16), 3441.

Wang, J., T. Sun, B., Liu, Y., Cao., Wang, D. (2018). Financial Markets Prediction with Deep Learning, 17th IEEE International Conference on Machine Learning and Applications (ICMLA), Orlando, FL, USA, 2018, pp. 97-104

Wang, J. (2023). Optimization of quantitative investment strategies in the financial big data environment. Frontiers in Business Economics and Management, 12(2), 52-54.

Wang, Z., Qiao, Y., Huang, S., and Liu, H. (2021). Cvar prediction model of the investment portfolio based on the convolutional neural network facilitates the risk management of the financial market. Journal of Global Information Management, 30(7), 1-19.

Zaar, A., Benaya, N., Moubtahij, H., Bakir, T., Mansouri, A., Allati, A. (2023). Ethereum cryptocurrency entry point and trend prediction using bitcoin correlation and multiple data combination. International Journal of Advanced Computer Science and Applications, 14(5).

Zhang, Z. (2023). Comparison of LSTM and ARIMA in price forecasting: evidence from five indexes., Proceedings of the 2023 2nd International Conference on Economics, Smart Finance and Contemporary Trade (ESFCT 2023).

Algorithmic Strategies for Precious Metals Price Forecasting

Gil Cohen *

Abstract

This research is the first attempt to create Machine Learning (ML) algorithmic systems that would be able to trade automatically precious metals. The algorithm uses three forecasts' methodologies: Linear regression (LR), Darvas Boxes (DB), and Bollinger bands (BB). Our data consists of twenty years of daily price data of five precious metals futures: Gold, Silver, Copper, Platinum, and Palladium. We found that all examined precious metals' current daily returns are negatively autocorrelated to their former day's returns and identified lagged interdependencies among the examined metals. Silver futures prices were found to be best forecasted by our systems and Platinum the worst. Moreover, our system better forecasts price-up trends than downtrends for all examined techniques and commodities. Linear Regression was found to be the best technique to forecast Silver and Gold prices trends while the Bollinger Band technique best fits Palladium forecasting.

Keywords: Precious Metals, Gold, Silver, Algorithmic Trading, Futures.

* Gil Cohen, Western Galilee Academic College, POB 2125 Acre, 2412101, Israel.

1. Introduction

The use of Artificial Intelligence (AI) in financial assets price forecasting and trading have become more and more frequent as the amount and speed of the flow of new financial data has increased dramatically. Algorithms are used to analyze simultaneous multi-sourced data. Those systems are developed by market experts and are usually applied to stocks and currencies markets. The following research develops and test such AI system and applies them to precious metals' future market. Precious metals have always been perceived by investors as a hedging tool against inflation (see for example Chebbi,2020) or stock market crashes. Gold and Silver are the leaders of that market followed by Copper, Platinum, and Palladium. Precious metals prices fail most tests of unbiasedness and are poor predictors of subsequent price changes but energy and agricultural futures fare much better. These findings of Chin and Coibion (2013) motivated us to search for algorithmic systems that will be able to predict future prices of precious metals for a substantial period of time. For that reason, we designed and optimized three algorithmic trading systems suitable for precious metal futures trading. Our system is based on advanced trading strategies that have never been examined before for such a long period of time on precious metal futures and it is based on technical analysis and market behavior. The Technical analysis approach, commonly used by practitioners to trade stocks and foreign exchanges, relies on historical data for the sake of forecasting future prices. We used Particle Swarm Optimization (PSO) algorithm as our primary optimization tool because of its ability to handle multi- objective optimization simultaneously.

Many researchers have tried to prove the ability of such algorithmic trading systems to achieve abnormal returns for stocks, currencies, and indices. However, not much evidence has been gathered concerning algorithmic trading systems designed for futures in general and particularly precious metals futures. The following research wants to fill that gap by an insight into three algorithmic trading strategies that were programmed and in accordance with the uniqueness of the precious metal financial markets. We use twenty years of futures daily data of five major precious metals including Gold, Silver, Copper, Platinum, and Palladium to test three algorithmic trading strategies: Linear Regression (LR), Darvas Boxes (DB), and Bollinger Bands (BB). We followed Cohen (2020) that concluded that LR and DB can help traders predicts the Bitcoin short-term price trends. Our 20 years of data were split into 10 years of training and optimization and 10 years of testing the trading results. We find that it is possible to forecast short-term price trends of precious metals. Silver futures prices were found to be best forecasted by our systems and Platinum the worst. Our system better forecasts price-up trends than downtrends for all examined techniques and commodities. Linear Regression was found to be the best technique to forecast silver and gold prices while the Bollinger Band technique best fits Palladium forecasting.

2. Literature Review

One important aspect of Machine Learning (ML) developed in recent years is pattern recognition. Bishop (2006) argued that Bayesian methods have grown from a specialist niche to become mainstream, while graphical models have emerged as a general framework for describing and applying probabilistic models. Moreover, the applicability of Bayesian methods has been greatly enhanced through the development of a range of approximate inference algorithms such as variational Bayes and expectation propagation. An important foundation for learning an input-output mapping from a set of examples was presented by Poggio and Girosi (1990). They developed a theoretical framework for the approximation method based on regularization networks that are closely related to pattern recognition. Their methodologies included task-dependent clustering and dimensionality reduction. Other researchers have provided an understanding of the mathematical concepts behind forecasting methods that are based on probabilistic derivations. Martino and Read (2021) have provided a joint introduction to Gaussian Processes (GP) and Relevance Vector Machines (RVM- developed by Tipping (2001) for regression, including within this framework the tasks of filtering, smoothing, and interpolation. They found that RVMs allow the choice of more general basis functions whereas the behavior of the predictive variance is generally counterintuitive. On the other hand, GPs present a good behavior of the predictive variance, but the choice of kernel functions is more restrictive .Candela (2004) has examined the GP and RVM models from a Bayesian perspective and concluded that probabilistic models have the important property of producing predictive distributions instead of point predictions. The researcher has also explored how to train systems with uncertain inputs and suggested that the first one tries to" guess "the unknown" true "inputs and requires careful optimization to avoid over-fitting and requires prior knowledge of the output noise, which is limiting. The second approach consists of sampling from the inputs posterior and optimizing the hyperparameters.

Most researchers that tried to explain precious metals prices have done so by linking the stock market to the precious metal market. Zheng (2015) for example, examined the relationship between aggregate stock market sentiment and metal futures returns and explained that precious metals futures have higher returns when investor sentiment is pessimistic rather than optimistic. Furthermore, metal futures return exhibit asymmetric responses to positive and negative investor sentiment shocks. Qadan (2019) has proved that investors' appetite for risk and the price of precious metals are highly linked. He argued that the price of precious metals and their volatility are driven by shocks originating in the economic uncertainty and risk appetite of investors that prevail in the equity market. Other researchers have focused on the interrelations between the prices of the leading precious metals. Sensoy (2013) showed that precious metals are strongly correlated with each other in the last decade which reduces the diversification benefits across them. Bosch and Pradkhan (2015) examined whether speculators positions predict returns and volatility in the precious metals futures markets. They found that weekly changes in traders' positions have a destabilizing impact on subsequent conditional volatility in gold, silver, and palladium futures markets.

Other researchers have linked precious metals prices to each other and to other commodities. Kang et al. (2017) examined spillover effects among six commodity futures markets – gold, silver, crude oil, corn, wheat, and rice. They found that both gold and silver are information transmitters to other commodity futures markets, while the remaining four commodity futures investigated were receivers of spillovers during recent periods of financial stress .Shahzad et al. (2019) have examined the impact of oil price changes on precious metals prices. They identified the safe-haven nature of precious metals against an oil price drop.

Past researchers have also attempted to construct AI systems to predict precious metals' prices. Alameer et al. (2019) proposed a hybrid model to provide an accurate model for forecasting the volatility of copper prices. Their model combines the adaptive neuro-fuzzy inference system and genetic algorithm. Cortez et al. (2018) argued that chaos theory and machine learning are able to identify the main variables affecting systems, recognize the relation and influence of variables through time, and discover hidden patterns governing systems evolution simultaneously. Unlike these attempts to predict precious metals prices, we designed algorithmic trading systems and tested their ability to predict precious metals prices.

3. Data and Methodologies

Our data consists of twenty years of daily data of open-close, high-low prices of five precious metals futures. We used lagged multi-dimension stepwise regression model to examined lagged correlations between the daily return of the examined precious metals including autocorrelations, as described in Equation 1.

$$(G,S,C,P,Pa)_i = \beta_1 G_{i=-1..-3} + \beta_2 S_{i=-1..-3} + \beta_3 C_{i=-1..-3} + \beta_4 P_{i=-1..-3} + \beta_5 Pa_{i=-1..-3} \quad (1)$$

Where: $(G,S,C,P,Pa)_i = the\ daily\ returns\ of$ Gold, Silver Copper, Platinum, and Palladium, $(G,S,C,P,Pa)_{i-1..3}$ is 1..3 days ago daily returns of Gold, Silver Copper, Platinum, and Palladium.

The results of this model enabled us to better understand short term autocorrelations of returns and lagged dependencies between the precious metals price movements and helped us design our trading systems.

3.1 Algorithmic Trading System

We design our algorithmic trading system to report the actual trading results: Net Profit (NP), Percent of Profitable trades of all trades (PP), and the Profit Factor (PF). NP is the dollar value of the total net profit generated by the trading system. The PP is the percentage number of winning trades out of the entire set of trades generated by the system. The PF is defined as gross profits divided by gross losses. We programmed three algorithmic systems based on three sophisticated trading technical tools and altered their configuration until we achieved maximum profitability in terms of NP and PF. The designed systems are based on three methodologies: Linear Regression, Darvas Boxes, and Bollinger Bands which are well-known technical formations that are commonly used to analyze investment opportunities for stock and currencies traders. We then optimized NP and PF by altering the setups behind our systems and splitting the system's performance into long and short positions.

The complexity of our systems needs a multi-objective optimization formulas. We selected Particle Swarm Optimization (PSO) which was developed by Kennedy and Eberhart (Kennedy and Eberhart (1995); Eberhart et al. (1996)) as our primary optimization method. This methodology enabled us to train the system in the initial period and test it in the latter period. The twenty years of our examined period was split into two separated periods, ten years of training and optimizing and ten years of testing and reporting results. The PSO uses a stepwise process to change the velocity of each particle toward its best location that maximizes our target function. We start the process with random particles that includes the trading time frames and the various tools ingredients. Next, for each set of particles, we evaluated the desired optimization fitness function using our predefined goals: Maximum Net Profit (NP), Profit Factor (PF), and Percentage of Profitable trades (PP). We then compared the fitness of the setups with "pbest"[3]. If the current value was better than "pbest," we set the "pbest" value to the current value. In addition, we compared the evaluations of the fitness of the setups with the population's overall previous best. If the current value was better than "gbest,"[4] we reset "gbest" to the current value and calculated the results according to Equation 2:

$$V\,(1)\; i{+}1{,}d = Vid + C1Rand * Pid - Xid + C2Rand\; Pgd - Xid \quad (2)$$

$$X\,(2)\; i{+}1{,}d = Xid + Vid \quad (3)$$

Where: Vid = *the value of each particle of the setup, Rand = random number,* Pid = *the particle's initial identification and* Pgd = *the particle's global best identification.*

Last, we looped the process using Equation 3 until the highest multiple objectives were achieved. The use of a random variable in the above process is essential for keeping the optimization process unbiased and to ensure that all variables have an equal chance of entering the process.

3.1 Linear Regression Strategy

Figure 1 demonstrates how we use the Linear Regressions technique for algorithmic trading platforms.

---

[3]*"pbest"* = The setup that achieved the best results in reducing the maximum drawdown and maximizing the percentage of profitable trades, the profit factor, and the net profit.

[4]*"gbest"* = global best identification.

Figure 1: Linear Regression Algorithmic Trading Strategy

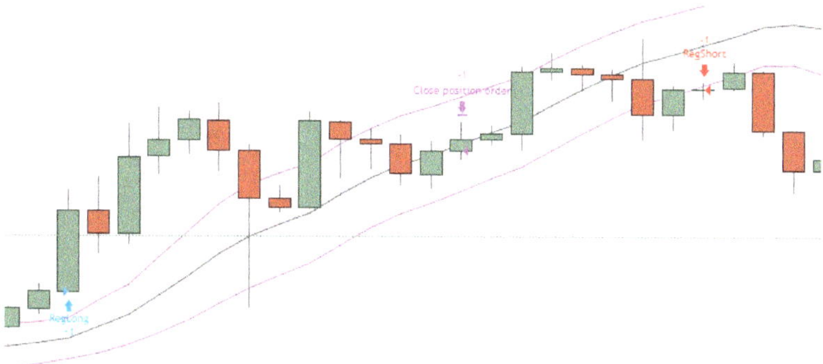

Notes: Every candlestick in Figure 1 represents the high/low open/close of the commodity futures daily prices. The middle line in Figure 1 represents the Linear Regression line while the other two lines represent one standard deviation from it.

When designing and deploying a Linear Regression strategy, one must first determine the length of time for the construction of the regression line. Second, the designer must decide about the span from that line that determines the entry and exit from the trading positions. The regression line in Figure 1, for example, is based on 50 trading days when one standard deviation from that line determines the entry and exit points to the trading position. When the actual price drifts upward from the +1 standard deviation line the system enters a long position that ends when the price crosses down the regression line. We started our PSO procedure by a random variable for both the daily time length and for the span that determined the actual entry and exits of trades. The system has altered those variables in order to maximize our trading targets.

3.2 Darvas Boxes Strategy

Figure 2 shows an example of an automated trading platform using Darvas Boxes.

Figure 2: Darvas Boxes Algorithmic Trading Strategy

Notes: Every candlestick in Figure 2 represents the high/low open/close Bitcoin daily prices. The green and red lines indicate the upper and lower boundaries of Darvas's Boxes.

Figure 2 shows how Darvas boxes are designed and how they generate a long and short signal. It is important to note that the trade signals symbolize a forecasted beginning of a price trend (up or down) based on the price breakout of the box designed with a predetermined number of days. The example presented in Figure 2 demonstrates an upward breakout which signals the beginning of a long trend and a down breakout which symbolizes the beginning of a downtrend. The long trend noted in Figure 2 continued for 50 days before a downtrend took place. This algorithmic trading system assumes that the trader is always exposed to price shifts between long and short positions. Darvas boxes use the notation that deviation from overtime horizontal support and resistance lines can be used to construct a winning trading strategy. The idea is that the asset's price should move within a specific box formation when no external news is provided and break formation when important news concerning the commodity is introduced to the financial markets. Boxes can be formed using any predetermined time frame according to the financial asset's volatility. A high volatility financial asset demands a shorter time frame box formation than a low volatility asset. The PSO process starts with a random number of days to construct the boxes and alter them to achieve better trading performances. Once the size and shape of the boxes are formed in the training period, it is used for the tested period for which performances are remeasured.

3.3. Bollinger Bands Strategy

Bollinger Bands (BB) was developed by famous technical trader John Bollinger. BB has plotted two standard deviations away from a simple moving average. The trading strategy that is demonstrated in Figure 3 uses 14 days for the moving average calculation with the original two standard deviations. When the price of the commodity crosses the lower band, the system opens a buy long order is placed, and when it crosses the upper band a sell short order is generated.

Figure 3: Bollinger Bands Algorithmic Trading Strategy

The PSO procedures starts with random setups for both the moving average and the standard deviations and optimize both particles of our trading system.

The three methodologies that were tested in this research are based on pattern recognition of price movements of the precious metals. The LR tries to adjust a linear model (horizontal or diagonal) to the data and determined price direction through a deviation from that linear formation. The DB methodology works on a shorter-term formation of boxes that represent the horizontal support and resistance lines. A deviation from that formation can be used to identify price trends shifts and support trading decision making. The concept that lies behind the BB structure does not demand the identification of a predetermined formation but rather determines a zone in which the financial assets are expected to move within a specific time frame. A break-out of the price from the expected zone can indicate irregularities of movements and can be used to make profits.

4. Results

We start the results section by presenting 10 years[5] monthly and daily correlations matrix between the returns of the examined precious metals.

Table 1: Correlations Matrix of Monthly and Daily Returns

	Period	Gold	Silver	Copper	Platinum	Palladium
Gold	M	1	0.75	0.25	0.51	0.28
Silver	M	0.75	1	0.45	0.61	0.44
Copper	M	0.25	0.45	1	0.56	0.51
Platinum	M	0.51	0.61	0.56	1	0.55
Palladium	M	0.28	0.44	0.51	0.55	1
Gold	D	1	-0.032	0.015	-0.015	-0.032
Silver	D	-0.032	1	-0.029	0.017	0.031
Copper	D	0.015	-0.029	1	0.015	-0.029
Platinum	D	-0.015	0.017	0.015	1	0.030
Palladium	D	-0.032	0.031	-0.029	0.030	1

From Table 1 we learn that all examine precious metal monthly returns are positively correlated. However, on a daily level, the correlations between the precious metals prices do not have the same sign. While Gold and Silver and Copper and Silver are negatively correlated, Platinum and Palladium and Silver and Platinum are positevelly correlated. We now apply to the daily data our designated multi-dimension regression model (Equation 1) and reporting the results for the standard stepwise regression model is presented in Table 2. This model enables us to better understand one untill three days lags dependencies of each metal to it's previous price changes and to the other precious metals.

[5] Until the end of April 2021.

Table 2: Results of the Regression Model

				Gold						
	G_{-1}	G_{-2}	G_{-3}	S_{-2}	S_{-3}	C_{-2}	C_{-3}	P_{-1}	P_{-2}	
Coeff	-0.20*	-0.17*	-0.04*	-0.02*	-0.02*	0.02	0.04	0.03	0.04	$R^2 = 0.14$
T stat	-11.00	-9.48	-2.14	-2.82	-2.04	0.97	1.86	1.57	1.73	F=21.6
				Silver						
	G_{-1}	G_{-2}	G_{-3}	S_{-1}	S_{-2}	S_{-3}	C_{-1}	C_{-2}		
Coeff	-0.04	0.09*	0.06*	-0.48*	-0.26*	-0.14*	0.26*	0.06		$R^2 = 0.19$
T stat	-1.18	2.44	1.82	-25.3	-12.36	-7.33	5.93	1.62		F=83.9
				Copper						
	G_{-1}	G_{-2}	G_{-3}	S_{-1}	S_{-2}	S_{-3}	C_{-1}	P_{-1}		
Coeff	0.01	0.01	-0.01	0.01	0.01	-0.02	-0.05*	0.02		$R^2 = 0.07$
T stat	0.75	0.72	0.73	1.26	0.15	-1.41	-2.42	1.14		F=2.7
				Platinum						
	G_{-1}	S_{-1}	S_{-2}	S_{-3}	C_{-3}	P_{-1}	P_{-2}	Pa_{-1}	Pa_{-2}	
Coeff	0.03*	0.11*	0.09*	0.04*	-0.02	-0.07*	-0.03*	0.09*	0.08*	$R^2 = 0.21$
T stat	1.95	14.65	10.65	5.60	1.27	-3.93	-2.05	6.73	5.85	F=39.4
				Palladium						
	G_{-2}	G_{-3}	S_{-1}	S_{-2}	S_{-3}	C_{-2}	C_{-3}	P_{-1}	Pa_{-1}	
Coeff	0.04*	-0.02	0.04*	0.01	0.02	0.02	-0.05	0.06*	0.08*	$R^2 = 0.15$
T stat	2.17	-1.04	3.78	1.39	1.75	0.76	-1.85	2.26	4.33	F=16.64

Notes: $(G,S,C,P,Pa)_i = daily\ returns\ of$ Gold, Silver Copper, Platinum and Palladium, $(G,S,C,P,Pa)_{i-1..3}$ is 1..3 days ago daily returns of Gold, Silver Copper, Platinum and Palladium. * = significant at 95% confidence level. R^2= the proportion of the variation in the dependent variable that is predictable from the independent variable(s). F=Statistic test results that measure the fitness of the model to the data. T stat=the ratio of the departure of the estimated value of a parameter from its hypothesized value to its standard error.

Table 2 show interesting phenomenon, all precious metals' current daily returns are negatively autocorrelated to their former days' returns. Gold and Silver to their former three consecutive days returns. Platinum to its two consecutive days returns and Copper and Palladium to their single former day returns. In terms of interdependencies, Table 2 exhibits that the Gold current daily returns are negatively affected by Silver's former days' returns. However, Silver's current daily returns are positively correlated to Gold's returns two and three days ago. Platinum's current daily returns have been found to be positively affected by Gold, Silver, and Palladium past returns. Palladium's current daily return was found to be positively correlated to yesterday's returns of Silver, and Platinum and two days ago of Gold's returns. The observations described above about the precious metals daily autocorrelations helped us better understand the flewency of daily prices to construct our trading strategy. All the designed trading systems are based on daily trading data. However, because of the different nature of these strategies, the number of days used for each of them which is determined solely by the optimization process is different. For example, the Linear Regression system needs more days than the other methodologies to construct its formations and therefore the algorithm needs a higher number of days to analyze the price trends and produce profitable trading signals than the systems that are based on Darvas Boxes and Bollinger Bands which are more dynamic in nature and therefore demand fewer days to achieve their best performances.

4.1 Linear Regression Trading Strategy

The Linear Regression strategy requires determining the number of days on which the Linear Regression line is formed. We start with a random number of days for each metal and optimize the trading results through our PSO system. The best trading results are summarised in Table 3 and Figure 4:

Table 3: Linear Regression Strategy Trading Results

Days		Gold	Silver	Copper	Platinum	Palladium
20	NP	53,390	315,150	72,612	-9,705	235,950**
	PP	45.48%	44.54%	43.88%	42.92%	40.67%
	PF	1.06	1.25	1.14	0.98	1.30
25	NP	90,680	415,175	122,662**	46,715	174,050
	PP	42.96%	44.18%	44.71%	43.5%	39.14%
	PF	1.13	1.40	1.22	1.10	1.23
	NP	159,810	600,750	121,450	51,955	-4,300

30	PP	45.55%	46.26%	43.87%	42.7%	39.7%
	PF	1.26	1.67	1.24	1.13	0.99
35	NP	171,040	589,150	112,862	73,445**	-133,650
	PP	43.89%	44.4%	44.41%	43.92%	8.8%
	PF	1.31	1.71	1.26	1.18	0.83
36	NP	165,180	558,975	119,837	59,225	-132,400
	PP	42.6%	43.91%	44.48%	43.25%	37.78%
	PF	1.30	1.64	1.28	1.15	0.83
37	NP	172,600	539,700	122,187	59,005	-159,950
	PP	42.63%	45.1%	44.65%	42.53%	37.76%
	PF	1.30	1.65	1.29	1.15	0.80
38	NP	177,190**	561,425**	96,737	40,110	-177,300
	PP	42.48%	44.15%	42.46%	41.72%	38.04%
	PF	1.32	1.69	1.22	1.09	0.78
39	NP	174,600	523,050	96,787	22,160	-219,000
	PP	43.78%	43.46%	41.62%	39.93%	37.09%
	PF	1.32	1.63	1.22	1.05	0.73
40	NP	167,460	480,000	79,400	27,700	-224,150
	PP	43%	41.64%	42.5%	40.14%	36.55%
	PF	1.31	1.58	1.18	1.069	0.73

Notes: NP=Net profit, PP=Percent of Profitable trades of all trades, PF=Profit Factor, Days= The number of Days on which the Linear Regression is constructed. **=The highest NP and PF, * The highest NP or PF.

Figure 4: Net Profits Trading Results of Linear Regression Strategy

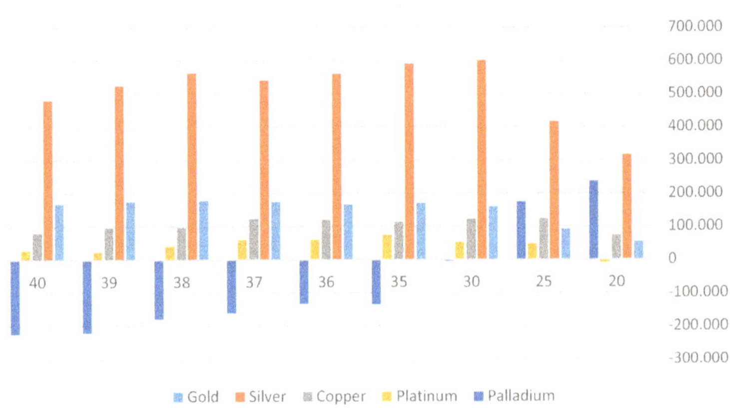

Table 3 and Figure 4 demonstrates that the Linear Regression methodology best fits to trade Silver, Palladium, and Gold and fits less to Copper and Platinum. The best setup for Gold and Silver trading systems is 38 days for which the system has

generated 177,198$ and 561,425$ NP, respectively. For palladium, the best setup is 20 days achieving an NP of 235,950$ with a PF of 1.30. In table 4 we split our trades into long and short trades to examine whether a difference in profitability will occur.

Table 4: Linear Regression Trading Results of Long /Short Strategies

Days		**Gold**	**Silver**	**Copper**	**Platinum**	**Palladium**
	NP	163,650	341,900	79,500	54,460	213,600
	PP	44.4%	45.6%	49.3%	46.5%	44.3%
Long	PF	1.6	1.82	1.39	1.3	1.67
	NP	13,540	219,525	42,687	18,985	22,350
	PP	41%	42.5%	39.8%	41.3%	37.3%
Short	PF	1.05	1.55	1.2	1.09	1.05

Notes: NP=Net profit, PP=Percent of Profitable trades of all trades, PF=Profit Factor. The results for Gold, Silver are calculated according to their optimum setups of 38 days, Copper 37 days, Platinum 35 days and Palladium 20 days.

Table 4 indicates that the Linear Regression technique fits both long and short trades. However, it is a better strategy for long trades than for short trades for all the examined commodities. The difference in long and short trades is significant for all metals in terms of NP and PF. Silver, again, is leading the other metals in both long and short trades, resulting in a PF of 1.8 for long trades and 1.55 for short trades.

4.2 Darvas Box Strategy

Darvas Box strategy requires determining the number of days on which the system will build the boxes formations and deliver buy or sell signals. Again, we start with a random number of days and let our PSO system to optimize our goal functions. The best trading results are summarized in Table 5 and Figure 5.

Table 5: Darvas Boxes Strategy Trading Results

Days		Gold	Silver	Copper	Platinum	Palladium
	NP	26,080	188,475	39,487	-12,725	-98,550
	PP	37.30%	36%	35.45%	37.8%	34.12%
5	PF	1.05	1.22	1.09	0.97	0.86
	NP	36,990	271,625	93,087	-42,775	-97,950
	PP	36.67%	36.24%	36%	37.9%	33%

6	PF	1.08	1.36	1.26	0.88	0.85
	NP	65,290**	319,200**	102,175**	-17,735	29,550
	PP	39.54%	37.75%	35.19%	36.36%	33.06%
7	PF	1.17	1.55	1.31	0.95	1.06
	NP	61,830	295,650	94,425	-29,445	36,750
	PP	38.49%	37.54%	37.81%	37.13%	33.18%
8	PF	1.17	1.55	1.31	0.91	1.07
	NP	-5,290	164,800	94,925	13,035**	21,150
	PP	36.33%	35.07%	40.11%	37%	33.51%
9	PF	0.98	1.28	1.35	1.05	1.04
	NP	13,610	111,125	55,662	-21,020	38,650**
	PP	33.62%	33.59%	38.79%	32.32%	33.14%
10	PF	1.04	1.19	1.20	0.93	1.09
	NP	2,500	191,875	35,412	-22,795	-26,250
	PP	35.61%	34.05%	39.1%	29.94%	32.7%
11	PF	1.00	1.38	1.13	0.92	0.94
	NP	-10,760	222,425	53,537	-40,555	-82,450
	PP	35.68%	36.89%	39.86%	29.7%	31.37%
12	PF	0.97	1.52	1.21	0.85	0.83
13	NP	-63,780	178,125	56,737	-17,490	-38,350
	PP	30.415	34 %	39%	30.61%	34%
	PF	0.83	1.39	1.24	0.93	0.91
	NP	-43,000	200,275	41,762	6,990	-14,950
	PP	32.15	35.71%	37.3%	32.33%	36.22%
14	PF	0.87	1.47	1.18	1.03	0.96
	NP	-122,000	148,125	29,212	10,590	-108,550
	PP	34%	32.56%	35.45%	31.93%	33.88%
15	PF	0.96	1.32	1.13	1.05	0.75

Notes: NP=Net profit, PP=Percent of Profitable trades of all trades, PF=Profit Factor, Days= The number of Days on which the Darvas Box is constructed. **=The highest NP and PF, * The highest NP or PF.

Figure 5: Net Profits Trading Results of Darvas Boxes Strategy

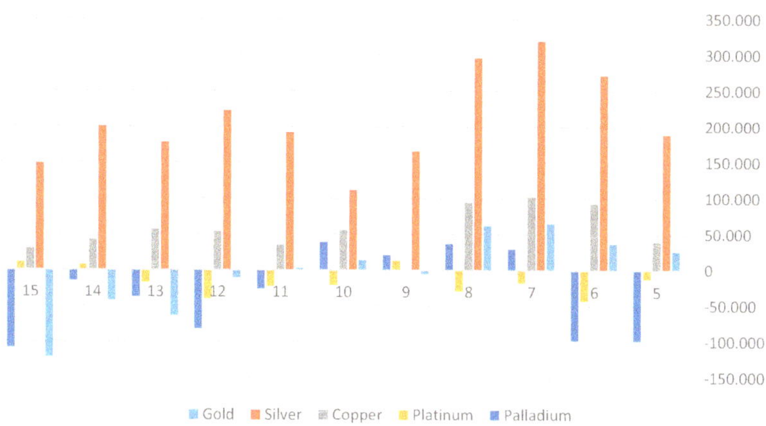

The trading results according to the Darvas Boxes methodology described in Table 5 and Figure 5 show that this methodology, like the Linear Regression technique, best forecasts silver price trends than copper and gold and it is less effective in forecasting future prices of Platinum and Palladium. Our system generated an NP of 319,200$ for silver, with a PF of 1.55, using a 7-day setup. This setup was found to be useful also for gold and copper trading. Table 6 divides all the trades into long and short trades using the optimized setups for each metal.

Table 6: Darvas Boxes Trading Results of Long /Short Strategies

Days		Gold	Silver	Copper	Platinum	Palladium
Long	NP	111,170	222,425	95,863	28,335	152,550
	PP	41.815	39.55%	39.32%	42.155	39.77%
	PF	1.77	1.93	1.79	1.28	2.02
Short	NP	-45,880	96,775	6,312	-15,300	-113,900
	PP	37.25%	35.96%	31.03%	31.7%	26.44%
	PF	0.81	1.28	1.03	0.91	0.58

Notes: NP=Net profit, PP=Percent of Profitable trades of all trades, PF=Profit Factor. The results for Gold, Silver and Copper are calculated according to their optimum setups of 7 days, Platinum 9 days and Palladium 10 days.

The table shows that for all five precious metals, the system again performed better for long trades than for short trades. Moreover, short trades have produced losses for Gold, Platinum, and Palladium. The only precious metals that Darvas Boxes technique fits both long and short trade are Silver and Copper. These results indicate that the system based on Darvas Boxes methodology can better predict positive future price trends than negative trends.

4.3 Bollinger Band Strategy

Table 7 summarizes the results of the examined metals prices using the Bollinger Band (BB) technique. This methodology calculates a moving average of a predetermined number of the trading day and contrasts the upper and lower bands using two standard deviations from that moving average. Using our PSO system we optimized the trading results for each commodity in terms of NP, PP, and PF. The results are presented in Table 7 and Figure 6.

Table 7: Bollinger Bands Strategy Trading Results

Days		Gold	Silver	Copper	Platinum	Palladium
	NP	-60	381,325**	12,462	-8,450	279,350*
	PP	60.2%	62.5%	64.7%	61.1%	56.1%
7	PF	1.0	1.67	1.03	0.97	1.80
	NP	37,470	248,425	-84,162	-80,850	311,950*
	PP	59.8%	61%	63.6%	63.3%	61%
8	PF	1.08	1.34	0.82	0.77	1.70
	NP	39,690	203,425	-89,450	-88,335	223,700
	PP	59.2%	63%	62.5%	65%	58.4%
9	PF	1.08	1.27	0.81	0.75	1.43
	NP	8,730	179,175	-90,262	-72,165	162,600
	PP	58.2%	65.5%	63.1%	65%	60%
10	PF	1.02	1.26	0.80	0.80	1.30
	NP	56,330	233,175	-64,937	-28,080	-118,800
	PP	60.6%	65.9%	62.4%	65.5%	57.9%
11	PF	1.13	1.35	0.85	0.92	0.80
	NP	69,310	61,925	-84,000	-31,120	-87,400
	PP	63.8%	65.9%	65.1%	66.5%	59.2%
12	PF	1.16	1.09	0.81	0.90	0.85
	NP	103,760**	7,100	-63,812	5,690	-116,000
	PP	63.7%	63.5%	65.6%	64.5%	58.7%
13	PF	1.25	1.01	0.85	1.02	0.79
	NP	88,190	-21,100	-68,412	-6,050	-22,100
	PP	63.6%	62.8%	64.3%	63.1%	59.6%
14	PF	1.22	0.97	0.83	0.98	0.96
	NP	83,580	14,950	-67,437	4,660	114,150
	PP	62.6%	64.3%	64.5%	65.6%	61.3%

15	PF	1.21	1.02	0.83	1.02	1.25
	NP	83,890	700	-4,562	6,300	104,650
	PP	63%	65.5%	66.7%	66.3%	60.8%
16	PF	1.21	1.0	0.98	1.02	1.24
	NP	77,980	67,225	-46,887	24,120	37,750
	PP	62.5%	66.1%	61.9%	66%	60.3%
17	PF	1.2	1.1	0.87	1.09	1.08
	NP	54,520	187,975	-13,837	28,780	33,950
	PP	62.3%	67.4%	63.8%	67.8%	62.3%
18	PF	1.14	1.33	0.96	1.11	1.07
	NP	48,340	280,495	59,812**	19,250	50,950
	PP	63.6%	67.5%	65.7%	68.8%	63%
19	PF	1.13	1.54	1.18	1.07	1.10
	NP	33,920	203,975	5,262	52,500**	10,550
	PP	61.2%	66.8%	65.8%	69.8%	62.9%
20	PF	1.09	1.41	1.02	1.19	1.02

Notes: NP=Net profit, PP=Percent of Profitable trades of all trades, PF=Profit Factor, Days= The number of Days on which the Bollinger Band is constructed. **=The highest NP and PF, * The highest NP or PF.

Figure 6: Net Profits Trading Results of Bollinger Bands Strategy

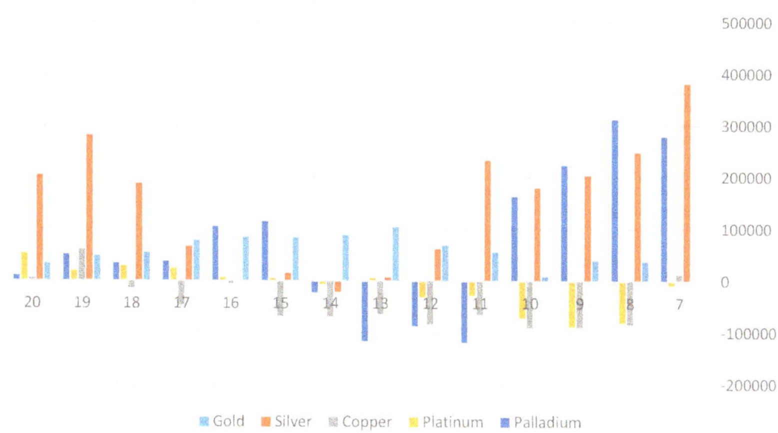

Table 7 and Figure 6 indicates that BB best forecasts Silver and Palladium future prices and it is less effective for Copper and Platinum. Seven days was found to be the best setup for Silver and Palladium while 13 days best fit the Gold price forecast. It is worth noting that Silver and palladium prices are more volatile than the other metals as was demonstrated in Table 1 resulting in relatively fewer preferred days setups for the BB methodology. The BB technique provided better Percent of Profitable (PP) results for all metals than the Linear Regression or the Darvas Boxes techniques making it the lowest risk algorithmic trading system. Table 8 splits the trades for long and short trades.

Table 8: Bollinger Bands Trading Results of Long /Short Strategies

Days		Gold	Silver	Copper	Platinum	Palladium
	NP	134,490	252,425	57,137	48,370	262,800
	PP	65.7%	63.5%	64.7%	73.2%	64.7%
Long	PF	1.85	2.12	1.37	1.35	2.65
	NP	-30,730	128,900	2,675	4,130	49,150
	PP	61.7%	61.5%	66.7%	66.4%	57.5%
Short	PF	0.88	1.37	1.02	1.03	1.17

Notes: NP=Net profit, PP=Percent of Profitable trades of all trades, PF=Profit Factor. The results for Gold, Silver and Copper are calculated according to their optimum setups of 7 days, Platinum 9 days and Palladium 10 days.

Table 8 indicates that again the BB methodology also fits better long than short trades. This technique fails to predict negative price trends of Gold.

5. Summary and Implications

In this research we examine the short-term behavior of five major precious metals and try to determine whether prices can be predicted and traded accordingly to algorithmic trading systems. By using a multidimensional regression model we found that all precious metals' current daily returns are negatively autocorrelated to their former days' returns. Gold and Silver to former three consecutive days returns. Platinum to two consecutive days returns and Copper and Palladium to a single former day returns. The model has also identified lagged interdependencies among the examined metals. These findings helped us to better understand the daily price fluctuation of each metal and to improve the trading systems. The trading systems using three forecasts' methodologies: Linear regression (LR), Darvas Boxes (DB), and Bollinger bands (BB). Our data consists of twenty years of daily price data of five precious metals futures: Gold, Silver, Copper, Platinum, and Palladium. During that long time, the precious metals have experienced high and low-price volatility under different economic conditions. We used PSO as our primary optimization tool because of the complexity of our target function. For that optimization process, we split our data into two equal time periods, ten years of training and optimization of our system and ten years of testing and reporting results.

We find that it is possible to forecast short-term price trends of all the examined precious metals. Moreover, we documented that our system better forecasts price-up trends than downtrends for all examined techniques and commodities. Our systems best predict Silver future prices and worst forecasts Platinum prices. Linear Regression was found to be the best forecasting technique of silver and gold price trends while the Bollinger Band best fits Palladium. This research has proven that precious metals prices can be predicted using an algorithmic trading system and therefore can be used by researchers, traders, and hedgers.

References

Alameer, Z., Elaziz, M.A., Ewees, A.A., Haiwang, Y., Zhang, J. (2019), Forecasting Copper Prices Using Hybrid Adaptive Neuro-Fuzzy Inference System and Genetic Algorithms. *Natural Resources Research*, **28,** 1385–1401.

Bosch, D., Pradkhan, E. (2015), The impact of speculation on precious metals futures markets, *Resources Policy*, 44, 118-134.

Bishop, C.M. (2006). Pattern Recognition and Machine Learning. Springer. Cambridge, U.K.

Candela, J.Q. (2004). Learning with uncertainty - Gaussian Processes and Relevance Vector Machines, *Technical University of Denmark*, 1–152.

Chebbi, T. (2020), The response of precious metal futures markets to unconventional monetary surprises in the presence of uncertainty, International Journal of Finance and Economics,*26,2,1897-1916.*

Chinn, M.D., Coibion, O. (2013), The predictive content of commodety futures, The journal of future markets, *34,7, 607-636.*

Cohen, G. (2020), Forecasting Bitcoin Trends Using Algorithmic Learning Systems, Entropy, *22(8), 838.*

Cortez,C. A. T., Saydam, S., Coulton, J., Sammut, C. (2018), Alternative techniques for forecasting mineral commodity prices, International Journal of Mining Science and Technology*, 28, 2, 309-322.*

Eberhart, R. C., Simpson, P. K., Dobbins, R. W. (1996). *Computational intelligence PC tools*. Boston: Academic Press Professional.

Kang, S.H., McIver, R., Yoon, S.M. (2017), Dynamic spillover effects among crude oil, precious metal, and agricultural commodity futures markets, *Energy Economics*,62,19-32.

Karanasos, M., Faek M.A., Zannis, M., Rajat, N. (2018), Modelling time varying volatility spillovers and conditional correlations across commodity metal futures, *International Review of Financial Analysis*, 57, 245-256.

Kennedy, J., Eberhart, R. C. (1995). Practical Swarm Optimization. In International conference on neural networks, *IV*, 1942–1948.

Li, J., Li, G., Yao, Y., Zhu, X. (2018). Identifying the influence factors of commodity futures market through a new text mining approach. In *The 7th international conference on futures and other derivatives*. Shanghai, China.

Martino, L., Read, J. (2021). Joint introduction to Gaussian Processes and Relevance Vector Machines with Connections to Kalman filtering and other Kernel Smoothers", Information Fusion, 74, 17-38.

Poggio, T., Girosi, F. (1990). Networks for approximation and learning, *Proceedings of the IEEE*, 78, 9, 1481–1497.

Qadan, M (2019), Risk appetite and the prices of precious metals, *Resources Policy*, 62, 138-153.

Shahzad, J.H., Rehman, M.U., Jammazi, R. (2019), Spillovers from oil to precious metals: Quantile approaches, *Resources Policy*, 61, 508-521.

Sensoy, A. (2013), Dynamic relationship between precious metals, *Resources Policy*, 38, 4, 504-511.

Tipping, M. E. (2001). Sparse Bayesian Learning and the Relevance Vector Machine. *Journal of Machine Learning Research*. 1: 211–244.

Zheng, Y. (2015), The linkage between aggregate investor sentiment and metal futures returns: A nonlinear approach, *The Quarterly Review of Economics and Finance*, 58, 128-142.

Intraday Trading of Cryptocurrencies Using Polynomial Auto Regression

Gil Cohen

Department of Management, Western Galilee College, Israel.

** Correspondence Email: gilc@wgalil.ac.il.*

Abstract

This research attempts to fit a Polynomial Auto Regression (PAR) model to intraday price data of four major cryptocurrencies and convert the model into a real-time profitable automated trading system. A PAR model was constructed to fit cryptocurrencies' behavior and to attempt to predict their short-term trends and trade them profitably. We used Machine Learning (ML) procedures enabling our system to train using minutes' data for six months and perform actual trading and reporting for the next six months. Results have shown that our system has dramatically outperformed the naive B&H strategy for all four examined cryptocurrencies. Results show that our system's best performances were achieved trading Ethereum and Bitcoin and worse trading Cardano .The highest Net Profit (NP) for Bitcoin trades was 15.58% achieved by using 67 minutes bars to form the prediction model compared to -44.8% for the B&H strategy. Trading Ethereum, the system generated 16.98% NP compared to -33.6% for the B&H strategy using 61 minutes bars. Moreover, the highest NPs achieved trading BNB and Cardano were 9.33% and 4.26% compared to 0.28% and -41.8% for the B&H strategy, respectively. Furthermore, the system has better predicted Ethereum and Cardano uptrends than downtrends while it better predicted Bitcoin and BNB downtrends than uptrends.

Keywords: Cryptocurrencies, Intraday Trading, Algorithmic, Artificial intelligence.

Mathematical Subject Classification: 37 A10, 37 D40

1. Introduction

Intraday trading is very short-term trading that is based on minutes of position holding and it is known to require special training and experience. Intraday trading can be performed manually or automatically using a preprogrammed algorithm that detects changes in a financial asset's pricing using Artificial Intelligence (AI) and machine learning (ML) techniques. Intraday trading challenges increase as the asset's volatility grows and demand algorithms with learning and optimization abilities. Because of their frantic price movement, not many researchers have attempted the challenge to develop and test intraday trading platforms for cryptocurrencies. In this paper we programmed, optimized, and tested the ability of Polynomial Auto Regressions (PAR) to successfully predict short-term price trends of cryptocurrencies that result in a profitable trading strategy. The cryptocurrencies that were used are Bitcoin, Ethereum, Binance Coin (BNB), and Cardano.

Artificial Neural Networks (ANN) are known to be able to provide an abnormal return by using technical indicators as predictors in stock markets (see for example Fischer and Krauss, 2018). Those methodologies were adopted by researchers to predict cryptocurrency future prices. Jay et al. (2020) predicted cryptocurrency prices using a stochastic model that induces layer-wise randomness into the observed feature activations of NN. Their results show that the proposed model can better predict cryptocurrencies' future prices than deterministic models. Senthuran and Halgamuge (2019) offered cryptocurrency price forecasting methodology using an ML algorithm and blockchain information. They concluded that prediction performance is high for both currencies when the blockchain data is used together with Bitcoin and Ethereum prices. Moreover, they documented that the Ethereum currency has the highest percentage of prediction accuracy and the lowest error rate compared to Bitcoin. NN uses learning filters that are generated in each of the network layers to detect a predetermined signal at any given layer and to send real-time information to the system that performs automated trading decisions. Shahariari et al. (2022) constructed ordinal partition network using price signals to investigate cryptocurrencies fluctuations. They investigated the premutation entropy and clustering coefficient and concluded that the global clustering coefficient using a minimum function for triplets in a loop in one direction has the highest predictive power.

In the current research, we used one year of minutes price data from the beginning of 1.12.2021 till the end of November 2022, to construct our trading platform. The data was split into six months of training and six months of actual trading and results reporting. We used ML procedures based on polynomial autoregression to predict the minute behavior of cryptocurrencies. The estimation of the parameters of the projected polynomial autoregressions is a non-linear least-squares problem. A PAR model for a stochastic process is defined in Equation 1:

$$X_{i+1} = \mu + \alpha X_i + \beta X_i^2 + \epsilon_{i+1} \tag{1}$$

Where: ϵ_i follows an independent distribution process with zero mean and finite variance.

The use of A PAR models to make a prediction is common in the scientific world because of their relative implementation simplicity compared to other non-linear models due to their parameter's linearity characteristics. PAR was used in a variety of academic fields such as communication (see for example Fernandes et al. 2010), biological control systems (see for example Gruber et al. 2010), and energy (see for example Hong et al. 2014). Karakuş et al. (2017) used Kuruoğlu (2002) model (presented in Equation 2), to predict the wind speed on the current day based on the previous day and concluded that the PAR model outperformed other models in both speed and power of predictions.

$$X(I) = \mu + \sum_i^k a_i^{(1)} x(I-i) + \sum_i^k \sum_j^k a_{i,j}^{(2)} x(I-i)x(I-j) + \cdots + \sum_{i,..}^{k,...} a_{i,...}^{(p)} x(I-i) \ldots + \epsilon(I) \tag{2}$$

Where: $\epsilon(I)$ is an independent and identically distributed sequence. P= the non-linearity degree, k= the Autoregression order.

PAR models are also used for financial research. De Luna (1998) argued that PAR could successfully be used to forecast time series trends. He used artificial Neural Networks (NN) to avoid an explosion of the parameters when considering a large number of lags. Furthermore, he demonstrated the methodology with real data for three-month US Treasury Bills. He concluded that that the stationarity of PAR is of no concern if they are considered not as models for stochastic process X_i but as approximation of the optimal predictor $E(X_{i+h} \vdots X_{i,....})$ defined by the minimum Mean-Squared Error (MSE) of prediction. They offered a family of predictors $X_{i+h}, h > 0$ and the model he used is described in Equation 3:

$$X_{i:h} = \beta_0 + \beta_1 X_i + \beta_2 X_{i-1} + \beta_3 X_i^2 + \beta_4 X_{i-1}^2 + \beta_5 X_i X_{i-1} \tag{3}$$

In practice, the optimal number of regressors can be decided using Machine Learning (ML) that searches for the best predictive model during the learning period. Moreover, in time series autoregression analysis a lag operator is needed to produce forecasts. A polynomial lag operator can be used within an ARMA (Autoregressive Moving Average) of orders p q (Equation 4).

$$X_t = \sum_{j=1}^{p} \emptyset_j X_{t-j} + \sum_{j=1}^{q} \theta_j \, \omega_{t-j} + \omega_t \tag{4}$$

In lag operator notation the ARMA process is define as:

$$\emptyset(B)X_t = \theta(B)\omega_t, t = 1, \dots., n \tag{5}$$

The characteristic polynomial can be expressed as:

$$\emptyset(B) = \prod_{i=1}^{p}(1 - \alpha_i B) \tag{6}$$

Were: α_i are the reciprocal roots.

In this research, we constructed an optimized trading platform using ML procedures. We aim to examine whether the polynomial model can fit minute data of cryptocurrencies, enabling the programmed trading platform to generate profits that outperform the simple Buy and Hold (B&H) strategy. We find that it is possible to intraday trade cryptocurrencies using a polynomial model. Our system has out beaten the B&H strategy for all examined cryptocurrencies.

2. Literature Review

ML has been used before to try to identify cryptocurrencies' price direction. Balcilar et al. (2017) discussed the predictability of Bitcoin returns and volatility based on transaction volume. They found that when extreme events are excluded, volume is an important predictor of price. In studying Bitcoin's price dynamics and speculative trading, Blau (2017) concluded that speculative behavior could not be directly linked to the unusual volatility of the Bitcoin market. Brandvold et al. Griffin and Shams (2020) examined whether Tether which is pegged to the U.S. dollar influenced Bitcoin and other cryptocurrencies prices during the 2017 boom. They found that Tether purchases follow market downtrends resulting in an increase in Bitcoin price. In addition, they suggested that there are insufficient Tether reserves before the month ends. Liu and Tsyvinski (2021) argued that cryptocurrencies' returns can be predicted by factors that are specific to the cryptocurrency market. They conducted a network factors analysis that captures the production along with the user adoption process of digital currencies and found that there is a strong time-series momentum effect and that proxies that capture investors' attention can forecast the future price trends of cryptocurrencies. Caporale and Plastun (2019) examined the day-of-the-week effect in the cryptocurrency market and found that most cryptocurrencies such as Litecoin, Ripple, and Dash do not exhibit this anomaly. The only exception is Bitcoin, for which returns on Mondays are significantly higher than those on the other days of the week.

Brandvold et al. (2015) investigated the role of various Bitcoin exchanges in the price discovery process, noting that the information shared is dynamic and evolves significantly over time. Feng et al. (2018) found evidence of informed trading in the Bitcoin market prior to major events. Moreover, when examining the timing of informed trades, they noticed that informed traders prefer to build their positions two days before large positive events and one day before large negative events. This result serves as proof of the market inefficiency that differentiates uninformed traders from informed traders of Bitcoin.

Some trading algorithms use only market data, and some combine market data with social media data (see for example Liu 2020, Sohangir et al. 2018). The social media information is extracted Mainly from Google and Twitter along with popular investors' idea exchanges platforms like Seeking Alpha[6] and Investopedia[7]. Since cryptocurrencies are relatively new, there is little research on the factors or tools that can help people invest in them. The first group of studies linked the price of Bitcoin to social networks. For example, Kim et al. (2016) tried to predict fluctuations in the prices of cryptocurrencies by analyzing comments in online cryptocurrency communities. They found that positive user comments significantly affected the price fluctuations of Bitcoin, whereas the prices of two other cryptocurrencies, Ripple (XRP) and Ethereum, were strongly influenced by negative user comments and replies. Garcia and Schweizer (2015) also demonstrated the existence of a relationship between returns and signals about the volume of trade, and Twitter valence and polarization. Matta et al. (2015) studied the existing relationship between Bitcoin's trading volumes and the number of queries on Google. They reported significant cross-correlation values, demonstrating that the volume of searches could predict the trading volume of Bitcoin. Detzel et al. (2021) examined trading strategies based on daily ratios of prices to their Moving Averages for Bitcoin and found that a trading strategy that is based on this concept beats the naïve strategy of Buy and Hold (B&H). Unlike Denzel et al. (2021) we use intraday data of five major cryptocurrencies. Shorter time frames have a different characteristic than daily data since they are not subjected to overnight new economic data. Moreover, intraday trading strategies should capture changes in the asset's price trends in shorter time frames measured in minutes not days. In addition, In the following research, we documented that the Relative Strength Index (RSI) based trading system has beaten the B&H strategy and can be used by intraday traders both human and robotic. Although the RSI and MA are both momentum oscillators, they measure different factors. The RSI uses average price gains and losses over a given period to indicate whether a security is overbought or oversold in relation to recent price levels while the MA-based strategy measures the current price against its periodic moving average.

Since financial asset price movements are very complex and affected by many factors, traders and researchers are using Support Vector Machines (SVM) for algorithmic detection of investment opportunities. The method that was developed by Vapnik (1995) is a machine learning technique based on statistical learning theory and structural risk minimization that is commonly used for classification (see for example Jan 2018; Xiao et al. 2020). In addition to SVMs,

---

[6] Seekingalpha.com

[7] Investopedia.com

Long-Short Term Memory (LSTM) is also being used for algorithmic trading because it can selectively decide whether historic data is important or not important as based information for future price forecasting (see for example Nelson et al. 2017. Borovkova and Tsiamas (2019) ensembled the LSTM model for intraday stock predictions, using a large variety of technical analysis indicators as network inputs. They evaluate the predictive power of our model on several US large-cap stocks and benchmark it against lasso and ridge logistic classifiers. The proposed model is found to perform better than the benchmark models or equally weighted ensembles. Fister et al. (2021) looked for a profitable trading strategy for stocks that experience low frequency release of new information. They formed LSTM networks that included trading patterns that are based on universal decision factors and stocks specific factors. They documented that their LSTM model significantly outperformed traditional trading strategies. Hansun et al. (2022) proposed three layers architecture for the regression prediction models. They found that LSTM and the Gated Recurrent Unit (GRU) have the same price prediction accuracy of major cryptocurrencies. However, in terms of execution speed, GRU is slightly better than LSTM. Oyedele et al. (2023) assessed the performance of Deep Learning (DL) models on six cryptocurrencies. Their results show that Convolutional Neural Networks (CNN) model has the highest explained variance score and lowest percentage error. They concluded that CNN models are reliable for cryptocurrency daily closing price prediction.

3. Data and Methodologies

Our data consists of twelve months' minutes' prices beginning at 1.12.2021, minutes bars[8] of the four most popular cryptocurrencies. The data was split into two periods: six months of training (December 2021-May 2022) and six months of actual trading and documenting the results (Jun 2022-November 2022). The autoregression model we used is described in Equation 7.

$$X_{i+1} = \alpha + \alpha_1(\beta_1 X_i + \beta_2 X_{i-n}) + \alpha_2(\beta_3 X_i + \beta_4 X_{i-n})^2 + \alpha_3(\beta_4 X_i + \beta_5 X_{i-n})^3 \quad (7)$$

Where: n= the number of minutes lag.

Our trading platform initially estimates and draws a polynomial model estimation line that best fits the data. Then, the system generates long and short signal according to the real-time price relative to the estimated line and enter trades accordingly. A long signal is generated when the price crosses the estimation line to the upside and a short signal is generated when prices cross the line to the downside. The methodology is illustrated in Figure 1.

Figure 1: Polynomial Autoregression Estimation Line and Long/Short Signals

To minimize false entries to a trade our system determined and optimized a minimum buffer above and below the prediction line (δ). The entry to a long/short position was defined in Equations 8 and 9.

---

[8] A Bar contains information about the open/close and high/low prices.

Long entry rule:

$$P_i > Pol_i + \delta \tag{8}$$

Short entry rule:

$$P_i < Pol_i + \delta \tag{9}$$

Where: P_i= the minute closing price, Pol_i=the polynomial prediction line, δ= minimum buffer.

Our starting point is a 100,000$ portfolio value enabling us to calculate the Net Profit (NP) Profit Factor (PF) and Percent of Profitable trades (PP) of six months of trading. Moreover, we calculate the percentage of returns and compare it to the simple Buy and Hold (B&H) strategy to examine the ability of our systems to outperform the B&H strategy. Moreover, we separated long from short positions to examine the abilities of the AI to trade profitably long versus short positions. The split between long and short trades was done for each cryptocurrency using the time frame that maximized NP.

NP is the dollar value of the total net profit generated by the trading system. The PF is defined as gross profits divided by gross losses. The result indicates the difference between the system's gains and losses. For example, if the profit factor is equal to 1.2, the system generated 20% more profits than losses. The PP is the percentage number of winning trades out of the entire set of trades generated by the system. If it is above 50 percent, the trading system has generated more winning trades than losing trades. However, this does not mean that the net profit of all trades is positive and vice versa. A score of less than 50 percent does not mean that the trading system is losing money. Although one might assume that the three profit indicators (NP, PF, and PP) move together, in fact, they can vary dramatically, and therefore may confuse investors and algorithmic traders. Each individual investor should pick at least one parameter as his/her target function according to the investor risk-averse level. For example, a more risk-averse investor will probably choose to maximize PP rather than maximize the NP while a risk seeker investor will prefer maximizing NP or PF as his/her primary target. The optimization process is presented in Figure 2.

Figure 2: The System Optimization Process

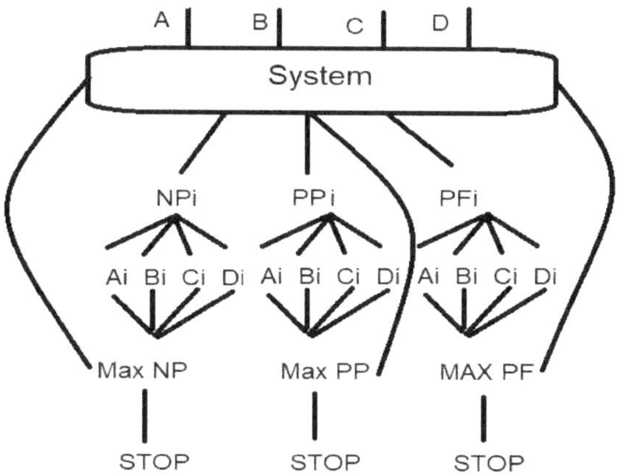

Figure 2 demonstrates that setups particles (A, B, C, D) are entered randomly into the system calculating initial NP, PP, and PF, then the system alters each particle at a time to reach the maximation of the target function. If the maximum is achieved the system halts, otherwise the setups particles are continuing to change. The system is trained to generate long and short signals in a sequence meaning that it will stay in a certain position (long or short) until an opposite signal appears.

4. Results

Our trading system has used six months of training to identify the best fit polynomial model for the examined cryptocurrencies. Moreover, the system has optimized the percentage deviation from the prediction line that will guide to enter a trade (long or short). In this regard, the optimal δ[9] was found to be 1.5 % for all four cryptocurrencies. Table 1 summarizes the trading performance according to our system for Bitcoin and Ethereum.

Table 1: Trading Results for Bitcoin and Ethereum

Minutes		Bitcoin	Minutes		Ethereum
	NP	876.8		NP	7,019
45	PF	1.05	45	PF	1.30
	PP	55.42		PP	56.63
	NP	4,991		NP	9,812
50	PF	1.35	50	PF	1.45
	PP	54.67		PP	56.16
	NP	5,792		NP	16,476
55	PF	1.43	55	PF	1.84
	PP	61.04		PP	60.56
	NP	8,549		NP	15,802
60	PF	1.67	58	PF	1.81
	PP	63.38		PP	61.19
	NP	12,355		NP	14,640
65	PF	2.04	59	PF	1.86
	PP	62.69		PP	61.54
	NP	14,940		NP	14,278
66	PF	2.09	60	PF	1.84
	PP	64.2		PP	61.9
	NP	15,580**		NP	16,980**
67	PF	2.30**	61	PF	2.04**
	PP	71.67**		PP	66.67**
	NP	15,003		NP	14,133
68	PF	2.11	62	PF	1.83
	PP	69.73		PP	66.62
69	NP	7,041		NP	9,532
	PF	1.53	65	PF	1.47
	PP	64.4		PP	56.63

[9] δ = the percentage gap from the prediction line.

70	NP	8,288	70	NP	12,505
	PF	1.72		PF	1.73
	PP	62.71		PP	60.38
75	NP	6,526	75	NP	10,706
	PF	1.56		PF	1.65
	PP	60.57		PP	58.9
80	NP	2,564	80	NP	8,408
	PF	1.23		PF	1.52
	PP	56.4		PP	56.7

Notes: NP=Net Profit, PF=Profit Factor, PP=Percent of Profitable trade of all trades. Minutes=the number of minutes trading bars used to form the prediction model. **= The highest score for each cryptocurrency. The results presented in the Table contain all trades including long and short trades.

Table 1 shows that the highest NP for Bitcoin trades 15,580$ (15.58%) was achieved using 67 minutes bars. This result dramatically outperformed the B&H strategy trading Bitcoin from the beginning of June 2022 till the end of November 2022 achieved -44.8%. The 67 minutes setup has also produced the highest FF (2.3) and PP 71.67%. The best NP for Ethereum trading was 16, 980$ (16.98%) compared to -33.6% for the B&H strategy using 61 minutes to form the best prediction line. This setup has also achieved the highest PF (2.04) and PP (66.67%). In Table 2 we separate long trades from short trades to be able to identify which price trend is better predicted by our system. Moreover, Table 2 reports the result of the trading using the best setup for each crypto (67 minutes for Bitcoin and 61 minutes for Ethereum).

Table 2: Long and Short Positions for Bitcoin and Ethereum

Position		**Bitcoin**	**Ethereum**
Long	NP	7,723	10,478
	PF	2.73	2.56
	PP	70	67.74
Short	NP	7,857	6,502
	PF	3.44	1.67
	PP	73.33	65.63

Notes: NP=Net Profit, PF=Profit Factor, PP=Percent of Profitable trade of all trades. For Bitcoin trading, 67 minutes setup was used and for Ethereum, 61 minutes setup. Long= an uptrend buy position. Short= a downtrend sell position.

Table 2 demonstrates that for Bitcoins trades the algorithm has achieved better results for short trades than for long trades. Short trades of Bitcoin have achieved

3.44 PF and 73.33% PP compared to 2.73 PF and 70% PP for long trades. With respect to Ethereum, the system better performed for long trades rather than for short trades, resulting in 10.478% NP compared to 6.5%. Table 3 shows the result of the optimized trading platform for BNB and Cardano trading.

Table 3: Trading Results for BNB and Cardano

Minutes		BNB	Minutes		Cardano
60	NP	-794	40	NP	-1,246
	PF	0.95		PF	0.90
	PP	56.25		PP	54.5
61	NP	684	45	NP	1,406
	PF	1.05		PF	1.12
	PP	58.82		PP	62.2
62	NP	9,330**	46	NP	1,211
	PF	1.75**		PF	1.10
	PP	67.6**		PP	62.8
63	NP	9,272	47	NP	4,259**
	PF	1.73		PF	1.38
	PP	65.6		PP	66.7**
64	NP	6,906	48	NP	3,406
	PF	1.54		PF	1.29
	PP	60		PP	65.12
65	NP	6,906	65	NP	2,946
	PF	1.54		PF	1.30
	PP	60		PP	63.3
70	NP	2,717	70	NP	3,010
	PF	1.19		PF	1.37
	PP	61.3		PP	58.3
75	NP	8,300	75	NP	3,676
	PF	1.65		PF	1.47**
	PP	65.5		PP	57.1
80	NP	2,047	80	NP	2,335
	PF	1.56		PF	1.26
	PP	52		PP	66.3

Notes: NP=Net Profit, PF=Profit Factor, PP=Percent of Profitable trade of all trades. Minutes=the number of minutes trading bars used to form the prediction model. **= The highest score for each cryptocurrency. The results presented in the Table contain all trades including long and short trades.

Table 3 demonstrates that the highest NP that was achieved trading BNB was 9,330$ (9.33%) using 62 minutes to form the polynomial prediction line compared to 0.28% NP for the B&H strategy at the same period. The best Cardano trading

NP was 4,259$ (4.259%) achieved using 47 minutes, while the B&B return was -41.8% during the same period. Table 4 is summarizing the results for long and short traded separately.

Table 4: Long and Short Positions for BNB and Cardano

Position		BNB	Cardano
Long	NP	1,386	2,326
	PF	1.16	1.39
	PP	58.8	73.9
Short	NP	7,944	1,933
	PF	3.05	1.35
	PP	76.5	59

Notes: NP=Net Profit, PF=Profit Factor, PP=Percent of Profitable trade of all trades. For BNB trading, 62 minutes setup was used and for Cardano,47 minutes setup. Long= an uptrend buy position. Short= a downtrend sell position.

Table 4 shows that the system performed much better for BNB short trades than for long trades, resulting in 7.94% of NP and 3.05 PF for short trades compared to only 1.38% NP and 1.16 PF for long trades. With respect to Cardano, the opposite has occurred. As for Ethereum, the system achieved better results in long trading Cardano than short trading, achieving 2.36 %NP and 1.39 PF for long trades compared to 1.93% NP and 1.35 PF, for short trades. Figure 3 is graphing the dollar value NP for the examined cryptocurrencies with respect to the number of minutes configurations of the polynomial model.

Figure 3: Net Profit and Number of Minutes Configuration

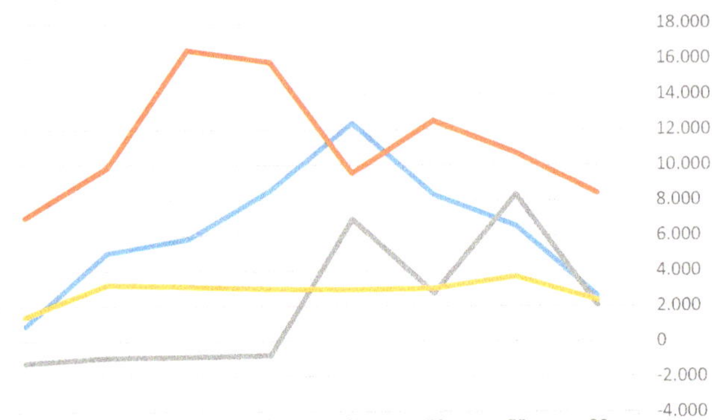

	45	50	55	60	65	70	75	80
Bitcoin	876,8	4.991	5.792	8.549	12.355	8.288	6.526	2.564
Ethereum	7.019	9.812	16.476	15.802	9.532	12.505	10.706	8.408
BNB	-1.213	-912	-870	-794	6.906	2.717	8.300	2.047
Cardano	1.406	3.201	3.112	3.002	2.946	3.010	3.676	2.335

Bitcoin   Ethereum   BNB   Cardano

Notes: The number of minutes represents the number of minutes bars that were used to construct the prediction model.

Figure 3 demonstrates that our system has achieved the best results trading Ethereum and Bitcoin and worse trading Cardano, however, as pointed out before, the system has outperformed the B&H strategy for all four cryptocurrencies. Figure 3 also points up that every crypto best-performing model relies on a different number of minutes. Moreover, three out of four currencies experience a signal peak performance while only BNB experiences double peaks at 65- and 75-minute models.

5. Summary and Conclusions

In this research, we attempted to fit a PAR model to minute price data of four major cryptocurrencies. The first intuition that raised this possibility is the visualization of the data that resembled a polynomial process. The challenge was not only to examine if a polynomial autoregression fits the data but to be able to convert it into a real trading algorithmic platform. We used ML procedures enabling our system to train for six months and perform actual trading and reporting for the next six months. Results have shown that for all four examined cryptocurrencies our system has dramatically outperformed the naive B&H strategy. Our system performed the best trading Ethereum and Bitcoin and worse trading Cardano. Trading Ethereum, the system generated 16.98% NP compared to -33.6% for the B&H strategy while trading Bitcoin the system generated 15.58% NP compared to -44.8% for the B&H strategy. Moreover, the system has located different best setups for each crypto. Furthermore, the system better performed Ethereum and Cardano long trades than short trades while it better performed Bitcoin and BNB short traded than long trades.

Acknowledgement

This research was support by Western Galilee Academic College.

Conflict of interests

The Author declare that he has no conflicts of interests.

References

Baek, C., Elbeck, M. (2014). Bitcoin as an investment or speculative vehicle? A first look. Applied Economics Letters, 22, 30–34.

Balcilar, M., Bouri, E., Gupta, R., et al. (2017). Can volume predict Bitcoin returns and volatility? A quantiles-based approach. Economic Modelling, 64, 74–81.

Blau, B. M. (2017). Price dynamics and speculative trading in Bitcoin. Research in Business Finance,41, 493–499.

Borovkova, S., Tsiamas, I. (2019). An ensemble of LSTM neural networks for high-frequency stock market classification. Journal of Forecasting, https://doi.org/10.1002/for.2585

Brandvold, M., Molner, P., Vagstad, K., et al. (2015). Price discovery on Bitcoin exchanges. Journal of international Finance Markets Institutions and Money, 36, 18–35.

Caporale, M. G., Plastun, A. (2019). The day of the week effect in the cryptocurrency market, Finance Research Letters, 31, 258–269.

Chow, Y. S., Robbins, H., Siegmund, D. (1971). Great expectations: The theory of optimal stopping. Boston, MA: Houghton Mifflin.

De Luna, X. (1998) Projected polynomial autoregression for prediction of stationary time series, Journal of Applied Statistics, 25:6, 763-775.

Detzel, A, Liu, H, Strauss, J, Zhou, G, Zhu, Y. (2021). Learning and predictability via technical analysis: Evidence from bitcoin and stocks with hard-to-value fundamentals. *Financial Management*. 50: 107– 137

Feng, W., Wang, Y., Zang, Z. (2018). Informed trading in the Bitcoin market. Finance Research Letters,26, 63–70.

Fernandes, C., Mota, J., Favier, G., et al. (2010). MIMO Volterra modeling for nonlinear communication channels. Learn. Nonlinear Models, 2, 8, 71–92.

Fister, D., Perc, M. & Jagrič, T. Two Robust Long Short-Term Memory Frameworks For Trading Stocks. Applied Intelligence. 51, 7177–7195

Garcia, D., Schweizer, F. (2015). Social signals and algorithmic trading of Bitcoin. R Soc Open Sci, 2, 9.

Griffin, J.M., Shams, M. (2020). Is Bitcoin Really Untethered? Journal of Finance 52, 57–87.

Gruber, J., Bordons, C., Bars, R., et al. (2010). Nonlinear predictive control of smooth nonlinear systems based on Volterra models. application to a pilot plant', Int. J. Robust Nonlinear Control, 20, 16, 1817–1835.

Hansun, S., Wicaksana, A., Khaliq, A.Q.M. (2022). Multivariate cryptocurrency prediction: comparative analysis of three recurrent neural networks approaches. Journal of Big Data 9, 50. https://doi.org/10.1186/s40537-022-00601-7

Hong, T., Pinson, P., Fan, S. (2014). Global energy forecasting competition 2012, Int. J. Forecast., 30, 2, 357–363.

Jan, C.L. (2018). An effective financial statements fraud detection model for the sustainable development of financial markets: evidence from Taiwan, Sustainability, 10, 2, 513.

Jay, P., Kalariya, V., Parmar, P., Tanwar, S., Kumar, N., Alazab, M. (2020) Stochastic neural networks for cryptocurrency price prediction. *IEEE* Access 8:82804–82818.

Karakuş ,O., Kuruoğlu, E.E., Altınkaya, M.A. (2017). One-day ahead wind speed/power prediction based on polynomial autoregressive model. IET the Institution of Engineering and Technology. 11,11, 1430-1439.

Kim, Y. B., Kim, J. G., Kim, W., Im, J. H., Kim, T. H., Kang, S. J., et al. (2016). Predicting fluctuations in cryptocurrency transactions based on user comments and replies. PLoS ONE, 11, 8.

Kuruoğlu, E. (2002). Nonlinear least LP-norm filters for nonlinear autoregressive α-stable processes. Digit. Signal Process. 12, 1, 119–142.

Liu, X. (2020). Target and position article - Analyzing the impact of user-generated content on B2B Firms' stock performance: big data analysis with machine learning methods, Industrial Marketing Management, 86, 30-39.

Liu, Y., Yang, A., Zhang, J., & Jingjing, Y. (2020). An optimal stopping problem of detecting entry points for trading modeled by geometric Brownian motion. Computational Economics, 55, 827–843.

Liu, Y., Tsyvinski, A. (2021). Risks and Returns of Cryptocurrency, The Review of Financial Studies. 34,6, 2689-2727.

Matta, M., Lunesu, L., & Marchesi, M. (2015). The predictor impact of Web search media on Bitcoin trading volumes. In 7th international joint conference on knowledge discovery, knowledge engineering and knowledge management.

Nelson, D.M.Q., Pereira, A.C.M., de Oliveira. (2017). Stock market's price movement prediction with LSTM neural networks. *International Joint Conference on Neural Networks (IJCNN),* 1419-1426.

Oyedele, A.A., Ajayi, A.O., Oyedele, L.O., Bello, S.A., Jimoh, K.O. (2023). Performance evaluation of deep learning and boosted trees for cryptocurrency closing price prediction. Expert Systems with Applications, 213, C. https://doi.org/10.1016/j.eswa.2022.119233

Shahriari, Z., Nazarimehr, F., Rajagopal, K., Jafari, S., Perc, M., Svetec, M. (2022).

Cryptocurrency price analysis with ordinal partition networks, Applied Mathematics and Computation, 430. https://doi.org/10.1016/j.amc.2022.127237.

Senthuran, G., Halgamuge, M. (2019). Prediction of Cryptocurrency Market Price Using Deep Learning and Blockchain Information: Bitcoin and Ethereum, New York, NY, USA: Taylor & Francis, 349-364.

Sohangir, S., Wang, D., Pomeranets, A. *et al.* (2018). Big Data: Deep Learning for financial sentiment analysis. *Journal of Big Data* 5, 3.

Vapnik, V.N. (1995). The Nature of Statistical Learning Theory, Springer, New York, NY, USA.

Xavier, D.L. (1998). Projected Polynomial Autoregression for Predicting of Stationary Time Series. *Journal of Applied Statistics*, 25,6,763-775.

Xiao, C., Xia, W., Jiang, J. (2020). Stock price forecast based on combined model of ARI-MA-LS-SVM. *Neural Computing and Application*, 32, 5379–5388.

AI Models for Predicting Stock Returns Using Fundamental, Technical, and Entropy-Based Strategies: A Semantic-Augmented Hybrid Approach

Cohen Gil, Aiche Avishay and Eichel Ron*

Abstract

This study examines the effectiveness of combining semantic intelligence drawn from Large Language Models (LLMs) such as ChatGPT-4o, with traditional machine learning (ML) algorithms to develop predictive portfolio strategies for NASDAQ-100 stocks over the 2020-2025 period. Three different predictive frameworks Fundamental, Technical, and Entropy-based are tested through the examination of novel combinations of ML and LLM-derived semantic metrics. The empirical results reveal a considerable divergence in optimal blending methods across the methodologies; namely, the technical methodology exhibits the best performance when using only ML predictions, with around 1,978% cumulative returns with monthly rebalancing. In contrast, the Fundamental methodology achieves its full potential when it is based primarily on LLM-derived semantic insights. The Entropy methodology is improved by a balanced combination of both semantic and ML signals, thus highlighting the potential of LLMs to improve predictive power by offering interpretative context for complex market interactions. These findings highlight the strategic importance of tailoring the semantic-algorithmic fusion to suit the nature of the predictive data and the investment horizon, with significant implications for portfolio management and future research in financial modeling.

*The authors are members of Western Galilee Academic College School of Management. Corresponding author Cohen Gil; gilc@wgalil.ac.il

1. Introduction

In modern parlance, the blending of traditional investment techniques with Artificial Intelligence (AI) has emerged as a central factor in financial forecasting. The capacity of AI to sift through and pool vast amounts of structured as well as unstructured data has enabled researchers and practitioners to construct increasingly sophisticated models for forecasting stock returns. Of the core fields of financial analysis: fundamental analysis, technical analysis, and entropy or complexity modeling there is a growing realization that AI holds the key to bolstering predictive power by adding greater precision, flexibility, and context sensitivity (Dey, 2022; Kramer et al., 2023; Shi & Zhao, 2020). Basic analysis underlies long-run investment strategies, involving the evaluation of a firm's underlying value by scanning financial statements, economic factors, industry conditions, and macroeconomic conditions. Metrics widely used in that regard include price-to-earnings (P/E) ratios, return on equity (ROE), debt-to-equity ratios, and discounted cash flow techniques. While such metrics provide important visibility into a firm's operational feasibility and long-run prospects, conventional basic analysis has come under criticism on account of its reliance on history and its lack of quick responsiveness to changes in conditions in the marketplace (Mokhtari, 2021). The application of AI to basic analysis through machine learning and language processing enables real-time evaluation of earnings releases, managerial statements, and macroeconomic discourse, thus providing a more dynamic and forward-looking analysis framework (Agusta et al., 2024; Zhou & Faff, 2016). At the same time, technical analysis inevitably remains a data-driven approach, focused on sentiment in the movement of price, volume, and market indications to predict short-run movements. Moving averages, Bollinger Bands, MACD, and Relative Strength Index (RSI) are tools that help traders identify changes in momentum, reversals, and support/resistance. While technical analysis excels in recognizing patterns of market dynamics, it has long been criticized for its limited explanatory powers and its inability to account for the broader market context (Dawson & Steeley, 2003). More recent developments in artificial intelligence, notably through deep learning methods, have greatly expanded the accuracy and automation of technical analysis by uncovering complex nonlinear relationships and enabling the identification of patterns through copious amounts of time series data. The implications of these advances have led towards improved real-time decision-making powers and greater responsiveness within high-frequency trading environments.

Alternative methods for forecasting stock returns include fuzzy logic, which represents a powerful tool for treating the ambiguity and uncertainty of financial variables. Although not a substitute for binary logic, fuzzy logic enables reasoning for situations where variables cannot be clear-cut either true or false but are situated on a continuum of truth values. This property makes fuzzy systems especially effective for assessing investor sentiment, speculative economic predictions, and imperfect market indicators. The Mamdani and Sugeno models, as well as the hybrid neuro-fuzzy methodologies like ANFIS, have been widely applied in financial forecasting, leading to improved precision under conditions of noise and non-linearity (Hurriyati et al., 2023; Alizadeh et al., 2010). When coupled with artificial intelligence and entropy-based approaches, fuzzy logic uncovers deeper insight into market intricacies, turbulence, and behavioral dynamics features typically ignored by rigid deterministic approaches. Ayyildiz and Iskenderoglu (2024) found that artificial neural networks, logistic regression, and support vector machine algorithms could predict the directional movements of all countries' stock indices with an accurate rate of over 70 percent. The researchers pointed out that the lack of economic indicators, the study time frame, and the number of technical tools used are limitations to their work.

Previous research shows that machine-learning models can forecast stock returns using fundamental, technical, and entropy-based features. To our knowledge, no study has yet embedded large-language-model (LLM) representations within each of these feature sets or measured the incremental contribution of the LLM layer to each strategy individually. This paper is the first to present a hybrid AI framework that combines the semantic context captured by transformer-based LLMs with conventional machine-learning pipelines for stock-return prediction.

The results are astounding: our technical approach, optimized in a monthly rebalanced context, achieved a spectacular cumulative return of 1,978% over traditional benchmarks. More importantly, our Entropy approach, using fuzzy entropy for capturing the structural intricacies of the market, achieved a strong cumulative return of 701% through balanced weighting with artificial intelligence and machine learning ($w = 0.70$).

The findings of this research have several key implications. First, we demonstrate that semantic context inclusion significantly improves predictive quality in cases of ambiguity and complexity, as supported by primary narratives and entropy measures. Second, our findings confirm that the effectiveness of semantic artificial intelligence relies on methodological frameworks, and there is little extra value derived from extremely reactive, machine learning-optimized models, but considerable benefits are found with techniques that emphasize long-run goals and complexities. Third, we propose a scalable and modular approach that should help practitioners and researchers customize AI-augmented models for congruence with the strategic focus of their investment methodologies. Our findings provide strong empirical evidence for the prudent application of semantic-aware AI in financial modeling, supporting a shift towards contextually aware and multimodal investment approaches over established machine learning uses.

To ground our investigation, we focused on the NASDAQ-100 index, a data-rich, innovation-driven set of firms that offers both structured financial disclosures and abundant textual information for semantic analysis. The NASDAQ-100 presents an especially suitable environment for testing LLM enhanced forecasting methods due to its concentration of well-documented, large-cap growth companies. We also chose the 2020–2025 time frame deliberately, as it captures a dynamic and uncertain period in recent market history, spanning the COVID-19 pandemic, inflationary surges, and monetary policy shifts. These conditions allow us to assess how hybrid semantic–algorithmic models perform not only in stable environments, but also under extreme and evolving market dynamics. From a practical standpoint, our models simulate stock selection within the index rather than replicating it, reflecting how active investors may apply AI-based tools in real-world decision-making.

2. Literature Review

The intersection of AI with fundamental and technical analysis has gained substantial scholarly attention, driven by its potential to enhance traditional forecasting frameworks. This section synthesizes key findings from recent literature, outlining how AI-based techniques augment conventional models across multiple investment approaches.

2.1 AI in Technical Analysis

The integration of AI into technical analysis has been widely studied, with consistent evidence supporting its predictive value. Souza et al. (2018) showed that AI-enhanced moving average strategies can outperform market averages in BRICS countries. Neely et al. (1997) demonstrated the viability of technical analysis using genetic programming in foreign exchange markets. While Dawson and Steeley (2003) reported mixed results on the predictive power of visual chart patterns in the UK, their findings highlight the context-specific nature of technical trading rules. Machine learning has become instrumental in enhancing technical indicators. Shi and Zhao (2020) used deep neural networks to model golden cross patterns, achieving superior predictive accuracy over a 10-year simulation. Yang and Hu (2022) further supported this direction, arguing that AI methods can successfully incorporate economic and political factors into technical analysis. Yoo et al. (2005) surveyed ML techniques that integrate event-driven variables, showing that qualitative information can enhance the technical framework. In line with this literature, our study demonstrates that ML-driven technical strategies excel under short-term rebalancing conditions, with the highest cumulative return (1,978%) observed in our monthly-optimized configuration. However, unlike previous studies, we also test the added impact of semantic enrichment and find minimal marginal benefit in the purely technical context, reaffirming that traditional technical models may already capture most short-term signals efficiently. Abraham et al. Abraham et al. (2022) propose utilizing a genetic algorithm combined with a random forest classifier to forecast daily stock trends. Their focus on predicting both uptrends and downtrends suggests that different algorithms might have varied efficiency depending on prevailing market conditions. Kabbani and Usta (2022), address stock trend prediction by integrating news sentiment analysis with technical indicators. Their methodology reinforces the notion that understanding market context (uptrend vs. downtrend) can significantly improve predictive capabilities. Like these researchers we reexamined the strategies during the stocks' downfall period. This stress-test analysis reinforces the internal robustness of the scoring framework and confirms that the performance reported in aggregate results does not reflect bullish trends. Instead, it includes genuine exposure to high-risk, high-uncertainty periods where market structure and investor behavior were highly disrupted, a critical benchmark for evaluating practical performance in real-world investment settings.

2.2 AI in Fundamental Analysis

Incorporating AI into fundamental analysis has yielded promising improvements in stock return prediction. Agusta et al. (2024) showed that recent financial indicators significantly improved the performance of MLP-based models. Zhou and Faff (2016) argued that combining cross-sectional and time-series fundamental data enhances predictive accuracy, while Mokhtari (2021) highlighted AI's ability to transform traditional approaches through adaptive learning from macroeconomic indicators. Our findings align with these studies but add a unique layer: the semantic AI augmentation of fundamental models was particularly impactful in our framework. AI-derived contextual interpretation of earnings calls, regulatory filings, and macroeconomic commentary enhanced the richness and timeliness of fundamental insights validating the critical role of unstructured data in long-term valuation.

2.3 Sentiment Analysis and NLP Applications

Sentiment analysis has seen rapid advancement through NLP models, enabling real-time monitoring of market mood. Liu et al. (2021) developed prompt-based NLP systems for low-data scenarios, while Yan and Wang (2024) proposed Attention-BiLSTM models to improve the granularity of sentiment prediction. Sufi and Khalil (2024) introduced high-accuracy multilingual sentiment monitors, and Yang (2023) demonstrated the profitability of analyst report sentiment tracking through hedged portfolios. Unlike prior work that isolates sentiment signals, our model integrates semantic indicators directly into scoring frameworks across all three investment strategies. This approach is particularly effective in Entropy-based models, where semantic inputs help contextualize complexity indicators—resulting in a well-balanced AI-ML hybrid that achieved a 701% cumulative return, demonstrating enhanced interpretability and resilience.

2.4 Fuzzy and Entropy-Based Approaches

Fuzzy logic and entropy models have gained prominence for their ability to capture the ambiguous and non-linear behavior of financial markets. Hurriyati et al. (2023) and Alizadeh et al. (2010) highlighted the strength of ANFIS in managing market uncertainty. Wu and Zhang (2019) introduced fuzzy entropy as a robust measure for comparing financial time series, while Zhou et al. (2015) demonstrated its utility in optimizing portfolios under uncertainty. Building on this, our Entropy strategy incorporates fuzzy entropy within a semantic-aware AI model, offering a novel synthesis that is not present in previous work. The results reveal that semantic context helps disambiguate complex structural signals, allowing for more stable performance in high-entropy environments.

2.5 Comparative and Hybrid Modeling

Finally, the growing demand for hybrid modeling is supported by studies such as Ramesh et al. (2023), who explored trust in AI-based robo-advisors, and Singh (2023), who showed AI's positive impact on financial performance. Zhao (2023) confirmed the effectiveness of adapting AI-based strategies to sentiment conditions supporting our finding that the optimal AI-ML blend depends on the investment horizon and strategy type. Our contribution extends this line of inquiry by empirically evaluating blended scoring models across three strategic axes, offering quantitative evidence of when and where semantic AI creates the most value. The result is a nuanced, adaptable framework that aligns model complexity with market complexity setting a foundation for the next generation of hybrid predictive systems in finance.

3. Methodology – LLM-Created Scoring Framework

This section outlines a series of predictive scoring systems that were designed and developed entirely by a large language model (LLM), ChatGPT-4o, to simulate how such a model might independently evaluate stock quality and return potential using structured financial data. The LLM did not rely on human defined investment heuristics or pre-existing financial models; rather, it selected the features, preprocessing steps, learning algorithms, and score transformations based on its autonomous interpretation of the problem. These scoring systems represent a novel form of collaborative machine-human research, in which the LLM serves not only as a computational assistant, but as an analytical architect.

The methodology is composed of three distinct strategies, each reflecting a different domain of financial reasoning. The first, *LLM-Constructed Fundamental Strategy*, focuses on extracting latent performance signals from company income statements. The second, *LLM-Constructed Technical Strategy*, identifies predictive patterns in price behavior and short-term return dynamics. The third, *LLM-Constructed Entropy Strategy*, approximates fuzzy entropy using volatility-based stability proxies. In each case, the scoring model is trained on forward-looking returns and updated monthly and quarterly across a rolling five-year prediction window, from 1.1.2020 until 1.1.2025. Final scores are normalized to the $[0, 1]$ interval and serve as the decision layer for the portfolio selection process.

3.1 LLM-Constructed Fundamental Strategy – Learning from Financial Performance Signals

The fundamental strategy is based on the premise that a firm's financial quality, as captured in its income statement, contains predictive information about future stock returns. Rather than relying on static, rule-based screens, we construct a supervised learning model to discover the implicit mapping between financial fundamentals and future performance. This allows us to capture complex, nonlinear interactions between accounting variables and market behavior.

We utilize quarterly income statement data for all NASDAQ-100 companies, obtained from Alpha Vantage, covering the period from 2019 through 2025. From these statements, we extract five features that capture profitability and operational efficiency: total revenue, operating income, net income, operating margin (operating income over total revenue), and net margin (net income over total revenue). These variables are chosen for their interpretability and established relevance in financial analysis.

Each data point is labeled with the corresponding 1-month and 1-quarter forward returns, based on adjusted close prices, forming two prediction targets for monthly and quarterly models respectively. The target return is always aligned with the most recent financial report available at the time of prediction, ensuring that our models mimic the information set accessible to real-world investors and avoid lookahead bias.

We employ a multi-layer feedforward neural network to learn the relationship between the five input features and forward returns. The network architecture consists of two hidden layers with 32 and 16 neurons respectively, using ReLU activation, and trained using the Adam optimizer with a maximum of 500 iterations. Data is normalized using a StandardScaler to improve convergence and comparability across features. The model is trained on a pooled panel of all tickers, allowing it to generalize across sectors while still capturing firm-level signals.

Model predictions are transformed into LLM-style scores by clipping the output to the $[0, 1]$ interval and applying percentile normalization where necessary. These scores represent the neural network's assessment of the relatively expected return of each stock, given its current financial condition. Separate models are trained for the monthly and quarterly horizons to reflect potentially different relationships between fundamentals and short-term versus medium-term returns.

3.2 LLM-Constructed Technical Strategy – Learning from Price Behavior and Return Patterns

The technical strategy focuses on extracting predictive signals from the time-series behavior of stock prices. Unlike the fundamental strategy, which relies on accounting data, this approach seeks to learn patterns in recent returns, momentum, moving averages, and volatility that may indicate directional persistence or mean reversion.

For each stock, we construct a set of features using daily adjusted close prices. These features include lagged returns over 1, 3, and 6-month windows; moving averages over 3 and 6 months; and realized return volatility over the same horizons. The features are computed by resampling the daily data at the beginning of each month (for the monthly model) or each quarter (for the quarterly model). To avoid instability due to missing values or illiquid stocks,

Forward returns over the next month and next quarter are calculated using the same price resampling method and used as labels for supervised learning. The feature set is standardized, and a Ridge regression model is trained to predict forward returns. Ridge regression is selected for its balance between interpretability and performance, and to mitigate overfitting in the presence of potentially collinear features.

Once trained, the model produces a score for each stock and date, which is normalized using a robust percentile-based method. Final technical scores fall within [0, 1] and represent the model's learned estimate of positive return momentum and price strength. These scores are updated monthly or quarterly depending on the portfolio rebalancing horizon and reflect evolving return structures across time.

3.3 LLM-Constructed Entropy Strategy – Approximating Predictability via Volatility-Based Models

The third strategy draws inspiration from the concept of fuzzy entropy, which quantifies the degree of uncertainty or disorder in a system. In financial markets, entropy-based models aim to identify stocks whose return dynamics exhibit high stability and low randomness, characteristics that are thought to be associated with more predictable and reliable performance.

To approximate fuzzy entropy in a data-driven way, we use rolling return volatility as a proxy for signal stability. Specifically, we compute the standard deviation of daily returns over 21-day and 63-day windows, which represent recent short- and medium-term return behavior. These features are updated monthly or quarterly to align with the rebalancing periods of our portfolio strategies.

The relationship between return stability and future returns is modeled using Ridge regression. As with the technical strategy, this choice provides interpretability and robustness against noisy or sparse data. The regression is trained using forward returns as the prediction target, and regularization strength is chosen via internal validation. By learning how recent return volatility relates to future performance, the model produces a score that captures the structure embedded in low-entropy price movements.

Predicted return scores are normalized to the $[0, 1]$ range, with higher scores corresponding to lower volatility and more predictable price behavior. This process operationalizes the entropy concept without requiring subjective membership functions or handcrafted thresholds. The resulting entropy-style score serves as a quantitative measure of signal clarity, suitable for integration into model-driven portfolio selection.

3.4. Construction of Algorithmic Scores and Hybrid Portfolio Optimization

This section outlines the construction of three machine learning–based predictive scoring systems for monthly and quarterly stock selection: one based on financial fundamentals, one on technical indicators derived from price dynamics, and one based on entropy-driven complexity analysis. Each strategy aims to extract a distinct informational signal from historical or structural properties of firms, allowing us to capture orthogonal alpha streams. These algorithmic scores are later blended with large language model (LLM) based scores, described earlier, to create hybrid stock ranking systems. The weights of these combinations are systematically optimized using historical return data.

The fundamental strategy draws on the well-established relationship between corporate performance and stock returns. For each company in the NASDAQ-100, we collected annual and quarterly financial statement data for a period of five years. The features extracted from each report included total revenue, gross profit, operating income, EBITDA, EBIT, net income, R&D expenditures, SG&A expenses, and interest-related metrics. From these, we derived financial ratios such as profit margins, operating leverage, R&D intensity, and return on equity. To mitigate the temporal sparsity of accounting releases, we added a feature encoding the number of days since the most recent report. This helped the models adjust confidence levels based on the freshness of the information.

A particularly innovative component of this strategy was the use of predictive modeling to estimate forthcoming report values before they were publicly released. We trained XGBoost regression models to predict each key financial metric using time series lags and trend-based features. XGBoost, an optimized implementation of gradient boosting, was selected for its ability to handle missing data, high-dimensional inputs, and complex nonlinear interactions without requiring heavy preprocessing. The model was trained on rolling windows, and predictions were generated recursively for each fiscal period to simulate a real-world forecasting scenario. These forward-looking fundamentals were then included in the feature set for a second layer of prediction, which estimated future stock returns over the next 21 or 63 trading days.

Once the enhanced feature set was finalized, combining both actual and predicted fundamentals, we proceeded to train a series of machine learning models to estimate forward stock returns. These return labels were computed over two investment horizons: 21 trading days (approximately one month) and 63 trading days (one quarter). To maintain consistency with real-world investment constraints, only data available up to the return prediction start date was used, and the forward returns were clipped to control for extreme outliers. This ensured that the learning process focused on realistic return behavior and mitigated distortions from one-off price shocks.

The core return prediction step involved training four distinct regression models: Ridge regression, XGBoost, Random Forest, and a multi-layer perceptron (MLP). Each model was chosen to capture a different structural view of the input-output relationship. Ridge regression provided a regularized linear baseline that handled correlated features well, which was particularly important given the use of overlapping financial ratios and forward-looking forecasts. XGBoost and Random Forest offered complementary tree-based approaches, the former optimized for complex, nonlinear interactions, and the latter for robust, variance-reduced predictions across noisy or heterogeneous firms. The MLP neural network introduced an additional layer of flexibility by modeling subtle nonlinear trends across the entire input space, especially when patterns were smooth but not easily captured by trees or linear models.

To ensure that each model was both stable and effective in its predictions, we applied tailored optimization procedures suited to the nature of each algorithm. Rather than performing exhaustive hyperparameter searches, we adopted a pragmatic approach that balances performance, generalization, and reproducibility.

For Ridge regression, we used the RidgeCV implementation, which automatically selects the regularization strength (alpha) by performing internal cross-validation. The candidate values tested were 0.1, 1.0, and 10.0, a range chosen to explore both light and moderate regularization. This allowed the model to adaptively control the influence of correlated features without discarding informative predictors, which is especially important when working with financial ratios and their forward-estimated counterparts that often move in tandem.

In the XGBoost model, we configured a conservative setup with 100 boosting rounds, a maximum tree depth of 3, and a learning rate of 0.1. These parameters were chosen to prevent overfitting while preserving the algorithm's ability to learn nonlinear and interaction effects. Since the feature set included both raw and derived metrics, this depth provided sufficient model complexity without compromising stability across different firms or time periods. The objective function used was squared error, aligning with our continuous return prediction targets.

For the Random Forest, we trained 100 decision trees with a maximum depth of 6. This relatively shallow depth was selected to avoid overfitting to firm-specific noise and to encourage general patterns to dominate across trees. Random subsampling and feature bagging were used by default, further reducing the risk of model variance and making the ensemble particularly well-suited for absorbing the irregularities present in financial data across firms and time.

The multi-layer perceptron (MLP) was configured with two hidden layers of 32 and 16 neurons respectively, using ReLU activation functions to introduce nonlinearity. The model was trained using the Adam optimizer, with a maximum of 500 iterations to allow for convergence without excessive training time. Preprocessing was handled using a "Standard-Scaler" within a pipeline to ensure that all input variables were appropriately scaled, a critical step in neural network training. The model also used a fixed random seed to maintain reproducibility and consistent convergence behavior.

Together, these carefully selected configurations allowed each model to contribute unique insights while maintaining overall robustness and compatibility within the ensemble structure.

To ensure stability and comparability across models, all inputs were standardized using "Standard-Scaler", and model outputs were transformed using a percentile-based normalization scheme. For each model, raw return predictions were scaled into the $[0, 1]$ interval after clipping values at the 1st and 99th percentiles. This allowed each model to contribute meaningfully to the final score without being skewed by scale or outliers. The normalized predictions were then blended using fixed weights: 30% each for Ridge and XGBoost, and 20% each for the MLP and Random Forest. These weights were selected based on internal validation and practical considerations of model diversity and risk control.

The result of this ensemble procedure is a single, unified score, the monthly (or quarterly) fundamental score, that reflects the synthesized view of multiple learning algorithms operating over a rich, forward-augmented fundamental dataset. This approach allows the strategy to dynamically respond to changes in firm fundamentals, both actual and anticipated, while leveraging the interpretability of structured financial features and the predictive power of diverse machine learning architectures.

The technical strategy employed a set of momentum and volatility indicators calculated from historical daily adjusted closing prices. Standard technical indicators such as Relative Strength Index (RSI), Moving Average Convergence Divergence (MACD), simple and exponential moving averages (SMAs, EMAs), and rolling standard deviation were used. These features were calculated over multiple windows (7, 14, and 21 days) to capture short-term and medium-term price dynamics. Rather than relying on a single predictive model, we adopted an ensemble approach comprising XGBoost, LightGBM, CatBoost, and an LSTM (Long Short-Term Memory) neural network.

Each model in the ensemble served a distinct purpose. The gradient boosting models (XGBoost, LightGBM, CatBoost) are tree-based learners that perform well with tabular data and are capable of modeling nonlinear interactions among features. LightGBM was particularly effective in high-dimensional settings due to its leaf-wise growth strategy and histogram-based feature binning. CatBoost was selected for its categorical feature handling and robustness against overfitting on small training sets. The LSTM, a type of recurrent neural network (RNN), was incorporated to learn from sequential dependencies in the input features. LSTMs are designed to preserve long-range memory through gated recurrent units, making them well-suited for modeling temporal dynamics and recurrent trends in financial time series. In our implementation, we trained LSTM models on 30-day rolling sequences of technical indicators and used them to predict 21- or 63-day forward returns. The outputs of all models were averaged to produce the final technical score.

The entropy strategy leverages fuzzy entropy, a nonlinear time series analysis tool that quantifies the degree of complexity or uncertainty in a system. Traditional entropy metrics such as Shannon entropy or approximate entropy require fixed-length sequences and suffer from sensitivity to noise or small fluctuations. Fuzzy entropy addresses these limitations by using a fuzzy membership function to determine the similarity between sequences. It replaces the binary similarity used in approximate entropy with a continuous-valued function, which reduces discontinuities and enhances robustness in noisy environments such as financial markets.

Mathematically, fuzzy entropy is calculated by first forming vectors $x_i \in R^m$ from a time series $X = \{x_1, x_2, \dots, x_N\}$ using embedding dimension m. For each vector x_i , the similarity to all other vectors x_j is measured using a fuzzy function

$$D_{ij} = exp\left(-\frac{(\|x_i - x_j\|^n)}{r}\right) \tag{1}$$

where r is a tolerance threshold and n is a fuzzification parameter (typically set to 2). The average similarity is computed for all pairs, and the entropy is defined as the natural logarithm of the ratio of average similarities for vectors of length m versus $m + 1$. The final entropy value reflects how predictable local patterns in the data remain when extended by one period step.

In our implementation, we applied fuzzy entropy to rolling windows of 30 trading days for each stock, generating a dynamic sequence of entropy values over time. These values were used directly as features or in conjunction with other statistical summaries (mean, variance, trend) to form a predictive vector. As with the technical strategy, we fed this vector into the same ensemble of models (XGBoost, LightGBM, CatBoost, LSTM), each of which predicted expected returns over the next investment horizon. The ensemble output formed the entropy-based score for each stock.

After obtaining predictive scores from the three algorithmic strategies, we combined them with the LLM-generated scores using a linear weighted average. For each strategy, the final combined score was computed as:

$$CombinedScore_{i,t} = w \cdot MLScore_{i,t} + (1 - w) \cdot LLMScore_{i,t} \quad (2)$$

where w is a blending weight assigned to the ML score, ranging from 0 to 1 in increments of 0.05. For each candidate weight, we conducted a portfolio simulation across the full backtest period. On each rebalancing date (monthly or quarterly), we selected the top 10 stocks with the highest combined score, formed an equal-weighted portfolio, and held it for the corresponding horizon (21 days or 63 days).

The returns of these portfolios were recorded and used to compute performance statistics, including average return per holding period, standard deviation (volatility), Sharpe ratio (assuming a zero risk-free rate), and cumulative return. The blending weight that yielded the highest cumulative return was identified as the optimal value for each strategy and frequency. For each optimal configuration, we retained the full return time series and the set of selected stocks per rebalancing period.

This comprehensive approach allowed us not only to compare the standalone performance of each algorithmic strategy but also to quantify the added value of integrating LLM-derived semantic signals. It further enabled a systematic, data-driven selection of combination weights that maximize portfolio performance, offering a robust and extensible framework for hybrid investment strategies.

It is important to note that although our analysis is based on historical data from 2020 to 2025, the modeling process was designed to reflect real-time investment conditions. At each rebalancing point, models were retrained using only data available up to that date, and forward returns were aligned to reflect future performance. This rolling-window approach ensures that each portfolio decision was made using a realistic information set, avoiding lookahead bias and simulating out-of-sample behavior. While this validation framework improves robustness within the tested period, we recognize that full generalization to future or external markets would require further testing, a direction we highlight in the conclusion as a valuable opportunity for future research.

4. Results

This chapter provides a comprehensive comparison of the performance of three independent forecast methods Fundamental, Technical, and Entropy applied to NASDAQ-100 stocks for the five-year forecast horizon from 2020 through 2025. All three methods incorporate algorithmic scores generated from machine learning (ML) models together with semantic scores based on a Large Language Model (LLM). The weighting parameter (w) in our composite scoring system signifies the proportion assigned to forecasts based on ML, while the remaining proportion, $1 - w$, quantifies the degree of reliance placed on the interpretations derived semantically from the LLM.

Table 1: Optimal ML Weights, Risk-Return Metrics, and Cumulative Returns for All Strategy-Frequency Combinations (2020–2025)

Strategy	Frequency	ML Weight	Sharpe	Average Return	Volatility	Cumulative Return
Technical	monthly	1	0.6934	7.50%	0.1082	1977.71%
Entropy	monthly	0.7	0.4207	5.23%	0.1244	700.52%
Fundamental	monthly	0.15	0.5001	4.32%	0.0863	578.40%
Technical	quarterly	0.45	1.2967	24.99%	0.1927	573.37%
Entropy	quarterly	0.4	0.6048	20.25%	0.3348	534.36%
Fundamental	quarterly	0	0.4899	14.71%	0.3002	326.12%

The results presented in Table 1 show substantial differences in the optimum machine learning weight (w) between methodologies and rebalancing frequencies, that is, between monthly and quarterly. The Technical approach performed best under monthly rebalancing conditions when solely based on machine learning predictions ($w = 1$), with a cumulative return of around 1,978% over the course of the study. The Fundamental approach, by way of comparison, performed best on a monthly basis with a machine learning weight of only 0.15, highlighting the substantial benefits of employing scores based largely on semantic large language models (LLMs). The Entropy method, which evaluates the fundamental attributes of stock price movements, performed best with an equal weighting approach ($w = 0.70$), thus highlighting its improved predictive power through a hybrid scoring framework that combines the sophisticated analyses of both machine learning and LLM approaches.

The examination of the quarterly rebalancing horizon highlights the crucial importance of successfully blending algorithmic and semantic scores. Compared with the quarterly technical approach, maximum performance was achieved using a machine learning weight of 0.45, yielding a total return of around 573%, coupled with a stellar Sharpe ratio of 1.297, the highest reported by any approach and time horizon. This report suggests that the addition of contextual intelligence from big language models significantly improves sustainability and reduces risk over long periods of investment without sacrificing significantly in terms of return. By comparison, the Entropy approach had the most impressive performance in the quarter with an equivalent intermediate machine learning weight of 0.40, indicating that the blending of semantic analysis and entropic metrics uniformly improves predictive effectiveness over long time periods. It should be noted that the Fundamental quarterly approach performed optimally with the most reliance on scores from big language models ($w = 0$), thus proving that semantic trackers associated with fundamental financial metrics occasionally perform better than structured algorithmic designs over extended horizons.

Figure 1: Cumulative Return Over Time for Top Monthly Strategies; Fundamental, Technical, Entropy

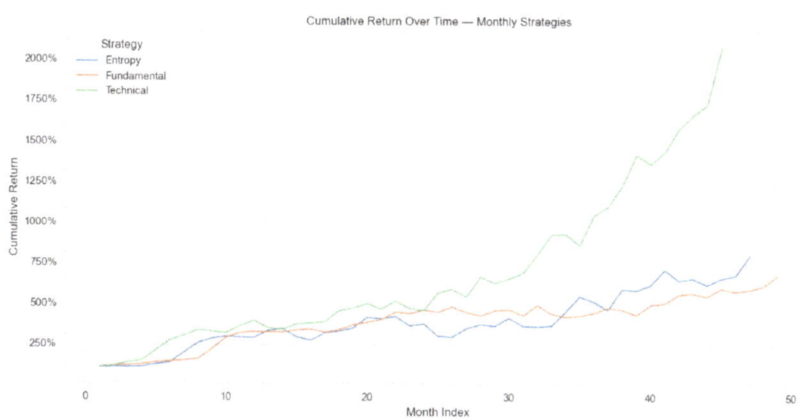

The cumulative return trajectories illustrated in Figure 1 offer deeper insight into the month-by-month evolution of the monthly strategies. Early on, all strategies exhibited relatively similar performance; however, after approximately two and a half years (around month 30), the monthly technical strategy diverged significantly upward, vastly outperforming its Fundamental and Entropy counterparts. This pronounced divergence emphasizes the technical strategy's ability driven purely by ML to effectively exploit momentum, trend-following, and short-term market inefficiencies. In contrast, the more balanced Entropy strategy and heavily semantic-driven Fundamental strategy demonstrated steadier but less explosive growth, suggesting that the value of semantic context and complexity measures lies more in risk moderation and stable incremental gains rather than aggressive return generation.

Figure 2: Monthly Return Volatility of Top Monthly Strategies by Method

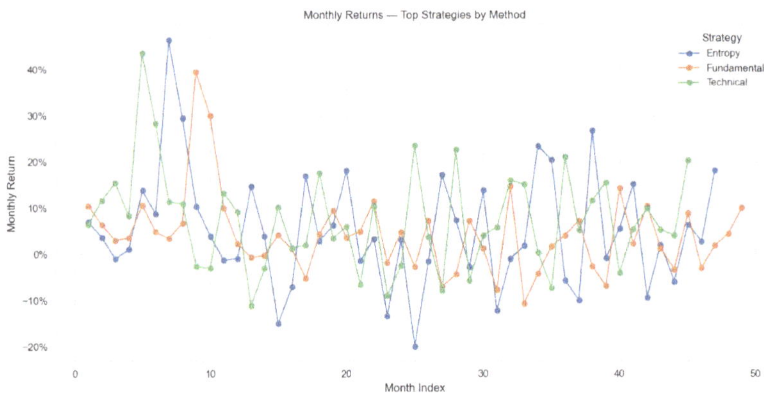

The month-to-month return variation presented in Figure 2 provides further insight. The Technical approach clearly displays higher volatility reflecting the higher, more aggressive nature of pure machine learning methods that take advantage of rapid market movements. The Fundamental approach, on the other hand, reflects less monthly volatility, reflecting its more conservative, fundamentally based approach augmented with the semantic understanding provided by the large language model. The Entropy approach falls in between, reflecting the optimal balance of machine learning parameters that determine its equilibrium between return and volatility, reflecting effective blending of market structure analysis with semantic context.

Figure 3: Cumulative Return as a Function of ML Score Weight (w) for Each Strategy

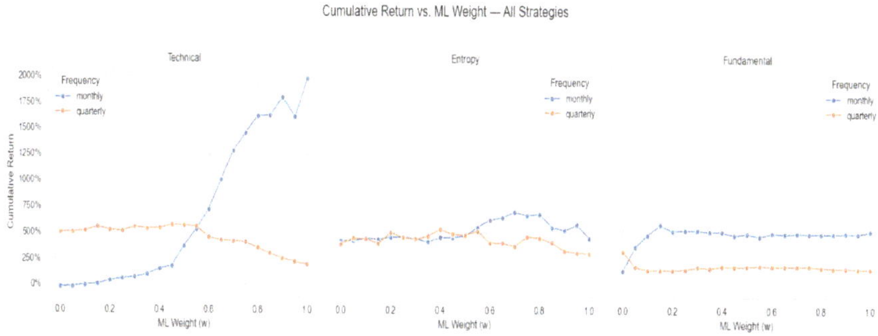

The analysis of cumulative returns over various machine learning weights (w), as plotted in Figure 3, reveals interesting results regarding optimal blending approaches for each methodology. The Technical method returns rise steadily in tandem with increasing ML weights, reaching 1 for monthly and 0.45 for quarterly measurements, respectively, thus clearly showing its affinity with quantitative, price-based modeling methodologies. The near-total dependence on ML for monthly Technical suggests minimal incremental benefit from semantic analysis in the context of short-horizon technical trading setups. In sharp contrast, the Entropy method manifested a clear concave relation, indicating diminishing returns at both extremes. Optimal performance was seen in a finely balanced mix of semantic inputs, revealing that large language model inputs materially enhance predictive power when analyzing intricate market dynamics. The Fundamental strategy shows a very different profile, with returns rising sharply to their peak at lower ML weights, reflecting the profound influence that semantic interpretations can exert over conventional financial fundamentals. Indeed, in the case of Fundamental analysis, the large language model's ability to contextually read earnings reports, management guidance, macroeconomic sentiments, and industry trends provides significant incremental predictive power over purely numerically driven algorithms.

Figure 4: Sharpe Ratio and Cumulative Return Comparison by Strategy and Frequency Monthly vs. Quarterly

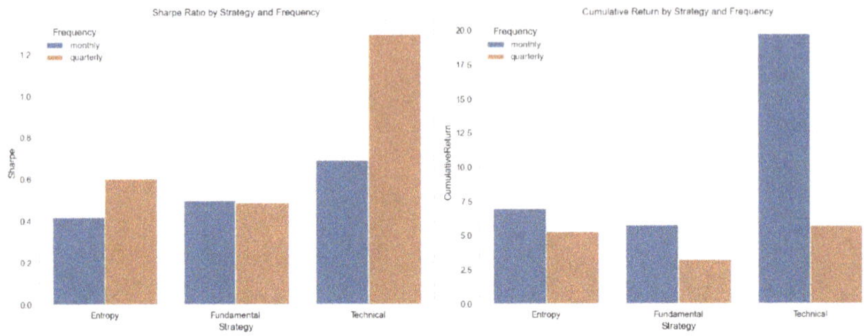

Figure 4, showing an overview of Sharpe ratios alongside cumulative returns for both the monthly and quarterly strategies, further substantiates these findings. It identifies the key risk-return trade-offs involved in the choice of strategies and machine learning weighting. Although the monthly technical strategy delivered impressive cumulative returns, its Sharpe ratio was significantly weaker than that of the quarterly version, reflecting an elevated relative risk. Conversely, the quarterly technical strategy, by virtue of its integrated nature, maximized risk-adjusted returns, thus supporting the fact that semantic insights, when coupled with algorithmic models, not only render predictive precision but also successfully reduce investment risk over extended holding periods. Furthermore, both Entropy and Fundamental strategies registered improvements in their risk-adjusted metrics when semantic analysis made a major contribution, substantiating the fact that the inclusion of qualitative LLM insights tends towards greater investment stability and efficiency.

In summary, the extensive empirical analysis demonstrates that strategic integration of ML and LLM insights can significantly enhance portfolio management across varying investment horizons. Pure ML methods excel where price momentum and short-term quantitative signals dominate, whereas semantic LLM insights profoundly improve outcomes in areas where complex context and interpretation of unstructured data such as fundamental metrics and entropy measures are critical. These results reinforce the idea that the optimal balance between structured and semantic information depends strongly on the type of data and the temporal investment horizon considered, thus providing valuable guidance for investors and portfolio managers seeking to leverage modern predictive methodologies to maximize returns and optimize risk profiles.

4.1 Performance Under Market Stress: COVID-19 Crash Analysis

To evaluate model robustness under extreme market conditions, we isolate the early 2020 COVID-19 crash, a period of historic volatility and rapid market correction. Between February and March 2020, the NASDAQ-100 and broader indices experienced one of the fastest and steepest drawdowns in modern financial history, triggered by uncertainty around the pandemic and global economic shutdowns.

Figure 5: Cumulative Return Over Time for Top Monthly Strategies; Fundamental, Technical, Entropy, at the beginning of COVID – 19 pandemics

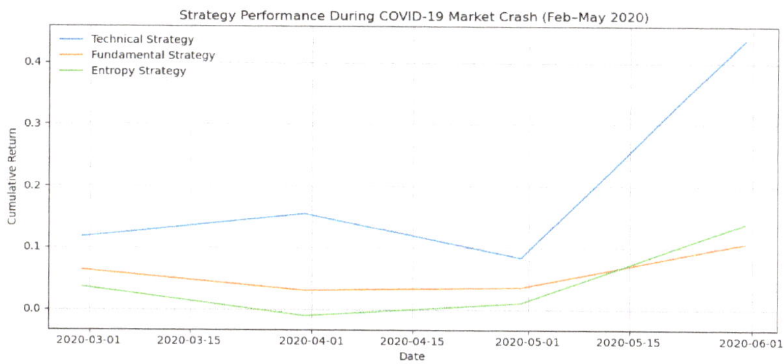

Figure 5 presents the cumulative return performance of the three strategy models, Fundamental, Technical, and Entropy, during the February to May 2020 window. The data clearly illustrates that all models encountered a turbulent environment, with sharp changes in momentum and volatility. Importantly, none of the strategies collapsed or ceased to function during this period, and all three displayed clear differentiation in behavior and recovery dynamics.

The Technical strategy initially outperformed during the early stages of the crash and was quick to rebound by May, suggesting its responsiveness to short-term price reversals. The Fundamental and Entropy strategies both showed more muted movements, reflecting a more conservative profile and perhaps some lag in adjusting to the new macroeconomic signals. Notably, while the Fundamental model exhibited a modest decline through March and April, it began to recover as forward-looking indicators stabilized, demonstrating the framework's ability to respond to changing market signals even under stress.

This stress-test analysis reinforces the internal robustness of the scoring framework and confirms that the performance reported in aggregate results does not merely reflect bullish trends. Instead, it includes genuine exposure to high-risk, high-uncertainty periods where market structure and investor behavior were highly disrupted, a critical benchmark for evaluating practical performance in real-world investment settings.

5. Concluding Remarks

The analysis demonstrates the tremendous potential of integrating ideas of Large Language Models with ordinary machine learning techniques in forecasting investments. By altering the ML weights of blended scoring techniques based on the application of Fundamentals, Technical analysis, and Entropy based techniques, we have provided strong evidence of when and where meaning contributes towards conventional numerical signals.

The Technical ML approach performed best on a monthly rebalancing schedule. It achieved returns around 1,978% in total. The Entropy approach was created to quantify the degree of market intricateness through fuzzy entropy calculations. It proved its worth through consistent and decent returns, totaling around 701% and equal weighting for ML and LLM ($w = 0.70$). The Entropy approach proved with ease that it could manage market intricateness. It demonstrated the significance of the concept of meaning in structural intricateness measurement, adding context that other simple approaches do not.

We see that the additional value of semantic context for using in LLMs varies greatly according to prediction method and horizon. Specifically, ML methods will work better in the short horizon when technical nuances and rapid shifts in data matter most. Conversely, the unambiguous benefit of semantic understanding demonstrates how semantic models can extract beneficial knowledge from verbose financial statements, major company announcements, and broad economic narratives.

The balanced optimization observed in Entropy strategies suggests that LLMs provide essential interpretive layers to market complexity measures, effectively bridging structural market indicators with sentiment and narrative information.

From a practical investment perspective, our results have clear implications. Portfolio managers focusing on short-term, momentum-driven strategies may continue relying on robust ML-based models, reserving semantic insights for tactical enhancements. In contrast, those emphasizing fundamental analysis should strongly consider allocating greater predictive responsibility to semantic-driven methods. For strategies grounded in market complexity and behavioral insights, hybrid models equally blending ML and LLM inputs appear ideal, offering an effective balance of precision and context.

Overall, this research illustrates the potential of semantic-aware machine learning in finance, advising practitioners and scholars to embrace hybrid predictive approaches that leverage the full analytical power of structured algorithmic methods alongside the interpretive capabilities of modern LLMs.

While the results are promising, it is important to acknowledge certain limitations. First, the study focuses on NASDAQ-100 stocks, which may limit generalizability to other indices or international markets. However, the methodology itself is adaptable to broader universes. Second, although our portfolio simulations are based on historical data, the use of rolling-window forecasting ensures that all predictions are made using information available at the time, thereby mimicking realistic, out-of-sample performance and avoiding lookahead bias. In addition to using a rolling-window forecasting framework, we further validated the robustness of our approach by isolating the COVID-19 crash period. This analysis, presented in Section 4.1, confirmed that the models remained functional and responsive even during one of the most volatile and uncertain market environments in recent history. The differentiated behavior across strategies during this period supports the view that the framework can adapt to dynamic market conditions, not just trending environments.

Compared to earlier studies like Ayyildiz and Iskenderoglu (2024), which focus on classification accuracy across indices, our work takes a more applied perspective by linking predictive outputs to actual portfolio construction. This enables us to assess not only the statistical strength of our models but also their investment utility over time.

Future research could extend this hybrid modeling framework to different markets, asset classes, or shorter holding periods. Practitioners may also explore how the integration of macroeconomic variables or real-time news sentiment impacts predictive performance. Ultimately, our study demonstrates how LLM-augmented models can bridge the gap between advanced AI capabilities and practical financial decision-making.

References

Abraham, R., Samad, M., Bakhach, A., El-Chaarani, H., Sardouk, A., Nemar, S., & Jaber, D. (2022). Forecasting a stock trend using genetic algorithm and random forest. Journal of Risk and Financial Management, 15(5), 188.

Agusta, S., Rakhman, F., Mustakini, J., & Wijayana, S. (2024). Enhancing the accuracy of stock return movement prediction in Indonesia through recent fundamental value incorporation in multilayer perceptron. Asian Journal of Accounting Research, 9(4), 358–377.

Alizadeh, M., Rada, R., Jolai, F., & Fotoohi, E. (2010). An adaptive neuro-fuzzy system for stock portfolio analysis. International Journal of Intelligent Systems, 26(2), 99–114.

Ayyildiz, N., & Iskenderoglu, O. (2024). How effective is machine learning in stock market predictions? Heliyon, 10(2): e24123.

Dawson, E., & Steeley, J. (2003). On the existence of visual technical patterns in the UK stock market. Journal of Business Finance & Accounting, 30(1–2), 263–293.

Dey, A. (2022). Machine Learning Algorithms: A Review. International Journal of Science and Research (IJSR). 11 (8), 1127-1133.

Hurriyati, R., Ana, A., Sulastri, S., Lisnawati, L., & Sawangsang, T. (2023). Stock market trend analysis and machine learning-based predictive evaluation. JOWUA, 14(3), 267–281.

Kabbani, T., & Usta, F. E. (2022). Predicting The Stock Trend Using News Sentiment Analysis and Technical Indicators in Spark. ArXiv. https://arxiv.org/abs/2201.12283

Kramer, B., Stang, M., Doskoc, V., Schäfers, W., & Friedrich, T. (2023). Automated valuation models: Improving model performance by choosing the optimal spatial training level. Journal of Property Research, 40, 365–390.

Liu, P., Yuan, W., Fu, J., Jiang, Z., Hayashi, H., & Neubig, G. (2021). Pre-train, Prompt, and Predict: A Systematic Survey of Prompting Methods in Natural Language Processing. ACM Computing Surveys, 55, 1–35.

Mokhtari, S., Kang. K & Yen, L.J. (2021). Effectiveness of artificial intelligence in stock market prediction based on machine learning. International Journal of Computer Applications, 183(7), 1-8.

Neely, C., Weller, P., & Dittmar, R. (1997). Is technical analysis in the foreign exchange market profitable? A genetic programming approach. Journal of Financial and Quantitative Analysis, 32(4), 405.

Ramesh, K. P., Amudha, R., Prasob, K., & Francis, J. (2023). Robo-advisory: An intrinsic convergence of AI in enhancing investment returns – An empirical analysis. Multidisciplinary Science Journal. 5, 2023ss0321.

Shi, M., & Zhao, Q. (2020). Stock Market Trend Prediction and Investment Strategy by Deep Neural Networks. 2020 11th International Conference on Awareness Science and Technology (iCAST), Qingdao, China, 1–6.

Singh, M. (2023). A Quantitative Study of Innovation-Driven Investment and its Performance Management on Corporate Fiscal Returns Using AI. 2023 12th International Conference on System Modeling & Advancement in Research Trends (SMART), 380–386.

Souza, M., Ramos, D., Pena, M., Sobreiro, V., & Kimura, H. (2018). Examination of the profitability of technical analysis based on moving average strategies in BRICS. Financial Innovation, 4(3).

Sufi, F., & Khalil, I. (2024). Automated Disaster Monitoring from Social Media Posts Using AI-Based Location Intelligence and Sentiment Analysis. IEEE Transactions on Computational Social Systems, 11, 4614–4624.

Wu, Z., & Zhang, W. (2019). Fractional refined composite multiscale fuzzy entropy of international stock indices. Entropy, 21(9), 914.

Yan, F., & Wang, J. (2024). Research on Sentiment Analysis of Micro-blog based on Attention-BiLSTM. Frontiers in Computing and Intelligent Systems. 7(3).

Yang, C. W. (2023). Investment strategy via analyst report text mining. Journal of Derivatives and Quantitative Studies. 31(2), 98-120.

Yoo, P., Kim, M., & Jan, T. (2005). Machine learning techniques and use of event information for stock market prediction: A survey and evaluation. International Conference (CIMCA-IAWTIC'06), Vienna, Austria, 835-841

Zhao, Y. (2023). Research on momentum strategy and contrarian strategy in AI stock prediction. Applied and Computational Engineering. 29, 125-132.

Zhou, Q., & Faff, R. (2016). The complementary role of cross-sectional and time-series information in forecasting stock returns. Australian Journal of Management, 42(1), 113–139.

Zhou, R., Zhan, Y., Cai, R., & Tong, G. (2015). A mean-variance hybrid-entropy model for portfolio selection with fuzzy returns. Entropy, 17(5), 3319–3331.

Appendix 2

The contribution of each explanatory variable to the accuracy of the random forest model is presented in the following table. Please note that the variables with the prefix *'l#_'* represents the number of lags taken on that particular variable. The "vix_dummy" is a dummy variable that receives "1" if the VIX index is greater than 20.

Variable	Contribution
Gold_MA_3	0.049966399
l1_GOLD	0.019207901
l2_GOLD	0.017918855
l1_ASX	0.002232515
l3_GOLD	0.002219208
l4_GOLD	0.001963917
l1_SP500	0.001531251
l1_TA35	0.001477213
l6_GAZ	0.001461528
l3_Usyield	0.001438446
l8_Silver	0.001395272
l1_IBEX	0.001273558
l5_N225	0.00124624
l1_AEX	0.00124352
l5_SMI	0.001188796
l7_N225	0.001165449
l6_Nifty	0.001159611
l7_SET	0.001112221
l9_FTSE	0.001100364
l9_Wheat	0.001091373
l7_Nifty	0.001089446
l7_BEL	0.001087911
l1_Usyield	0.001080972
l9_IBEX	0.001071255
l10_NZX	0.001054144
l2_Nifty	0.001053071
l2_N225	0.001050322
l6_BEL	0.00104733
l7_FTSE	0.001023262
l4_N225	0.001008689
l1_JAPANYield	0.001003315

l4_MOEX	0.001003264
l3_N225	0.000999807
l8_MOEX	0.000996453
l1_VIX	0.000984781
l5_BEL	0.000972938
l2_TA35	0.000961839
l10_DAX	0.000957736
l4_HIS	0.000941529
l4_BEL	0.00093914
l6_FTSE	0.000915598
l5_HIS	0.000900247
l3_BVSP	0.000889518
l2_NSDQ	0.000747899
VIX Dummy	0.0000542713

Note: MA

www.ingramcontent.com/pod-product-compliance
Lightning Source LLC
LaVergne TN
LVHW052322200926
848481LV00002B/647
9798899663437